Cambridge Elements ≡

Elements in Women Theatre Makers
edited by
Elaine Aston
Lancaster University
Melissa Sihra
Trinity College Dublin

THE THEATRE OF LOUISE LOWE

Miriam Haughton
University of Galway

CAMBRIDGE
UNIVERSITY PRESS

CAMBRIDGE
UNIVERSITY PRESS

Shaftesbury Road, Cambridge CB2 8EA, United Kingdom

One Liberty Plaza, 20th Floor, New York, NY 10006, USA

477 Williamstown Road, Port Melbourne, VIC 3207, Australia

314–321, 3rd Floor, Plot 3, Splendor Forum, Jasola District Centre, New Delhi – 110025, India

103 Penang Road, #05–06/07, Visioncrest Commercial, Singapore 238467

Cambridge University Press is part of Cambridge University Press & Assessment, a department of the University of Cambridge.

We share the University's mission to contribute to society through the pursuit of education, learning and research at the highest international levels of excellence.

www.cambridge.org
Information on this title: www.cambridge.org/9781009598385

DOI: 10.1017/9781009279512

First published 2025

A catalogue record for this publication is available from the British Library

ISBN 978-1-009-59838-5 Hardback
ISBN 978-1-009-27954-3 Paperback
ISSN 2634-2391 (online)
ISSN 2634-2383 (print)

The Theatre of Louise Lowe

Elements in Women Theatre Makers

DOI: 10.1017/9781009279512
First published online: March 2025

Miriam Haughton
University of Galway

Author for correspondence: Miriam Haughton,
miriam.haughton@universityofgalway.ie

Abstract: Louise Lowe is a theatre and performance director, writer, choreographer, dramaturge, and, more recently, a television director and short film writer/director, working in Ireland and internationally. She is the co-artistic director of ANU Productions, established with Owen Boss in Dublin in 2009. Lowe is known for facilitating and creating moments of interior reckoning for audiences through immersive performance techniques. These techniques engage spectators in affectively realised moments of understanding that the stories unfolding through performance reflect living histories in need of greater socio-political engagement and intervention. This Element assesses Lowe's creative practice and production history since her days as a drama facilitator in women's prisons and resource centres in Dublin, paying particular attention to the economic struggle of Dublin's north inner-city, the markings of which are potently visible in the work she makes, and how she makes it. This title is also available as Open Access on Cambridge Core.

Keywords: Louise Lowe, ANU Productions, Irish Theatre, Directing, Playwriting

ISBNs: 9781009598385 (HB), 9781009279543 (PB), 9781009279512 (OC)
ISSNs: 2634-2391 (online), 2634-2383 (print)

Contents

1 Introducing Louise Lowe   1

2 Staging Ireland's Nannies   21

3 Unfolding Women's Bodies from Ireland's Violent Past 41

References   63

1 Introducing Louise Lowe

'Poverty stings, under the skin, we can't be afraid to acknowledge it,' theatre artist Louise Lowe reflects in one of the many interviews undertaken since 2011 when I first encountered her work (Lowe and Boss, 2023). This study of Lowe's theatrical practice will be framed significantly by her personal experience of childhood poverty and its lifelong impact on her creative and social sensibilities. My very first interview with Lowe occurred after experiencing *Laundry* (Figure 1) in 2011 (ANU, directed by Lowe), a site-specific performance in Ireland's longest running Magdalene Laundry building located on Seán McDermott St Lower in Dublin's north inner city, formerly Gloucester St (ANU, 2011; Haughton, 2014a; Singleton, 2016). The most recent interview with Lowe occurred a few weeks prior to this Element's publication. Throughout those fourteen years in between, Lowe has emerged as Ireland's leading theatre director whose creative abilities extend beyond the traditional theatre roles such as 'director' and 'playwright', and the parameters we associate with them. Attempting to categorise or classify her roles or abilities will not produce any groundbreaking insights into her theatrical practice, motivations, or productions. Asking which role(s) she inhabits is not the right question for this study. Instead, asking where she is from and what she is driven by will bring us closer to understanding the work she makes, why she makes it and how she makes it. Essential to any study of Lowe's work is her primary experiences of community and care networks in Dublin's struggling north inner city and how these bonds activate her own vision for artistic encounters in contemporary society. Lowe's insights in this regard shape her work in direct and intense ways, which inform the research rationale and ideological structures underpinning this study.

Lowe wrote her first play *Diptych* in 1996 for Dublin Fringe Festival and the Belfast Festival at Queens followed by a national tour ('Louise Lowe', Irish Playography). Since then, Lowe writes, directs, and casts for theatre primarily with more recent professional commissions occurring in television and film. ANU Productions was formed and registered as a production company in 2009 by Lowe and Owen Boss as co-Artistic Directors, mirroring their now well-established reputation for collaborative practice in all aspects of their creative process. Lowe's contributions are most often captured in ANU's theatre programmes and publicity materials as a director and playwright, while Boss is often credited as set designer and visual artist. Both admit their nomenclature has never felt like a perfect fit, and they change their titles as the specific needs of any given production demands (Lowe, 2021b; Boss, 2024). For the first decade of ANU's work, Lowe rarely credited herself as the playwright in addition to the director, though in many productions, she was the first or primary

Figure 1 *Laundry* (2011). Performer Sorcha Kenny, Image by Pat Redmond.

writer of the script. However, the scripts she writes for ANU productions operate as moving documents, referred to as a 'show document' in rehearsals (Lowe, 2021a) which is regularly shifting, absorbing the contributions of performers, designers, production crew, or, indeed, anyone in the rehearsal room and performance space while the performance is being constructed, rehearsed, and revised (Boss, 2024). Furthermore, once the ensemble of performers is cast, the performers choose their own 'characters' which thus informs the shape and scope of the script further. Úna Kavanagh, a founding ANU ensemble member and regular performer, notes that the word 'character' does not fit right in her mouth (Kavanagh, 2024) most likely as the 'characters' are a selection of historical figures being re-presented in live performance encounters. Every narrative they recount and audible or physical suggestion they infer is developed from historical and archival records. In short, Lowe's work with ANU is rarely fictional in root and stem. The performers identify which historical figure they wish to bring to life as part of a sustained research phase of the rehearsal period. Following this, scenes can be formed, timed, and put into a rotation structure, as Lowe's work with ANU usually has a minimum of two starting points of approximately three to eight audience members per scene. Then, the dialogue can be firmly cemented alongside the embodied encounters, dance performance, live art, and installation art that are often essential ingredients of ANU's work.

This Element will assess Lowe's creative practice and production history since her early days as a drama facilitator in prisons and resource centres in her native Dublin, Ireland (1995–2000). However, as recognised from the outset, it is vital to open this study reflecting on how her own experience of childhood poverty is a fundamental part of her creative DNA. It was visible in *Laundry* (2011), the first ANU production directed by Lowe that I experienced, capturing the economic vulnerabilities of the women institutionalised throughout the twentieth century in Ireland as part of an oppressive and punitive culture dictated by a conservative Roman Catholic hierarchy. Their influence extended throughout the legal, civic, and bureaucratic apparatus of the newly formed Irish state (1921–1922), a state struggling for legitimacy and rendered vulnerable by centuries of poverty, colonialism, and war. The voices of those woman – poor, exploited, violated, and abandoned – remained silenced for almost a century in Irish public discourse (Smith, 2007; Haughton et al., 2021; McGettrick et al., 2021). *Laundry* remains part of my own DNA as a theatre scholar and audience member, marking a shift in my own critical and emotional capacities to invest in performance as world-making. The production confronted the various, distinct, and historically specific experiences of women and their families in granular detail with nuance and sensitivity, highlighting experiences rarely acknowledged officially for the majority of the twentieth and twenty-first centuries in Ireland. It remains embedded in memory for those who experienced it, established as a landmark moment in contemporary Irish theatre and performance. *Laundry* simultaneously communicated the complexities of institutionalisation in Ireland, and, re-asserted the role of the arts to symbolise, critique, engage, and inform a contemporary Irish society emotionally drained by decades of fiscal corruption (European Commission), weak governance, and bankrupt religious teachings (O'Toole, *The Guardian* 2018). However, while my own feminist connection to Lowe's work may be easily traced through her platforming of women's experiences, Lowe's primary artistic motivations are rooted in her own background and formative experiences submerged in the economic struggle of Dublin's north inner city, the markings of which are potently visible in the work she makes and how she makes it.

This following stark statistic is difficult to digest yet it captures the significance of Lowe's motivations and influences. In Lowe's final school class of eighteen students in 1992, six remain alive. Lowe discusses this with Irish drag queen and writer Panti Bliss in 2020 (Pantisocracy podcast/video), but three years later, that number has fallen to four (Lowe, 2023). In some parts of the country, Lowe argues a 'social genocide' has occurred that seems to have gone unnoticed (Pantisocracy). She emphasises 'poverty' with a sense of urgency when she speaks of it, which must be considered separate from standard definitions of 'working class' (Cambridge Dictionary), though she is highly attuned to class demographics in Irish theatre and beyond. Language – words such as poverty, class, and disadvantage – cannot fully capture her personal experience of childhood nor that of any individual, collective or group. It makes sense then that her work is so driven by physicality, choreography, and bodily intimacy, not only in its presentation to audiences but through its choreography of audiences as an essential aspect of her dramaturgy. Lowe stages stories by centring the bodies of her performers, audiences, and the communities in which her productions take place. This centring of the body simultaneously underwrites the potency and precarity of humanity, the impact and affect of which ripple outwards. According to Catriona Crowe, former Head of Special Projects at the National Archives of Ireland who has collaborated with Lowe and ANU on multiple commissions as part of Ireland's 'Decade of Centenaries 2012–2023' (DoC), Lowe has a unique capacity to confront the truth of complex past experiences, absorb them, and re-present them in performance in a way that does not detract from the pain, while enabling a cohesive encounter for audiences to engage with and, thus, examine (Crowe, 2023). Her method and style of 'confrontation' of seismic events are not didactic, Crowe asserts with great caution (Crowe). Rather, she envisions a diversity of experiences, facts, archival legacies, perspectives, and, indeed, contradictions to present distinct positions of a past event. Crowe's comments chime with ANU's consideration of 'Cubist dramaturgy – [by] exposing multiple sides and states simultaneously' (Kavanagh and Lowe 2017, p. 119). Lowe and Kavanagh, reflecting critically on ANU's creative process, explain the central contention of this dramaturgical approach:

> As much as possible, we try to avoid exposition, believing that its absence opens up a kaleidoscope of myriad possibilities. Deploying (on top of this),

a cubist dramaturgy – by exposing multiple surfaces and states simultaneously – we invite audiences to create their own multi-fractured narratives, becoming auteurs of their own instinctive experience ('The Work of ANU' p. 119–120).

Lowe's confrontation of the 'kaleidoscope of myriad possibilities' of historical narratives is a method of examining the past empathetically to come to terms with the present. The twenty-first century, thus far, remains as challenging economically, socially, and politically as the century previous. Yet, perhaps by confronting historical roots of injustice in intimate theatrical encounters for both audiences and performers, one might begin to reimagine the potential of the present moment that decouples the value of society from neoliberal priorities that continue to subsume national governance regardless of the social consequences. In short, there is no way to rationalise fourteen deaths from a class of eighteen coming of age approximately thirty years ago. There is only the opportunity to acknowledge it, examine it, and, indeed, question whether the root causes of such inequity have changed?

1.1 Co-Creation, Golden Tickets, and Ticking Clocks

Lowe's show documents are constantly subject to change. At final stages of rehearsal prior to previews, this document is often abandoned as the implicit understanding surfaces that it is no longer required (Haughton rehearsal notes, *The Wakefires* rehearsals 2022; *Hammam* rehearsals 2023). Durational, second-specific performance scenes transform from actions and lines that must be embedded into muscle memory as part of the performers', designers', and technicians' daily routine, logistically conceived, supported, and monitored by ANU stage manager and performer, Leanna Cuttle. Cuttle's role in the artistic, logistical, and communal development and presentation of ANU's performances, often invisible to the audience, is essential. If rehearsal of a scene results in a single-second overrun, Cuttle returns the company to first positions to start again, continuing to drill the performance until the exact timing is achieved. At this moment, the 'Clock is King' mantra takes hold. As one audience member or small group leaves an encounter, the next individual or group enters it, and thus, scenes cannot run over their allocated time. If an immersive encounter with an audience member takes up too much time or an error of some kind delays the scene's timing, performers must decide to cut something forthcoming to save the seconds that were lost. The 'Clock is King' policy must be adhered to in order to facilitate the full performance to unfold, thus ensuring time and space for the 'Golden Ticket'. The 'Golden Ticket' is where a performer invites a single audience member to learn something new that the remaining audience members do not learn, see or experience. As part of this one-to-one moment, they are removed temporarily from the audience grouping with whom they entered the performance space. Lowe asserts that 'it should matter that you're [the audience] there' (2013), and this philosophy manifests as a leading dramaturgical thread in all her work that is produced by ANU. Part of the 'Golden Ticket' concept is enabling the audience to 'feel, witness, comply or act' (Joye and Lowe 2015, p. 141) in response to provocations and invitations made by the company in performance. By ensuring time and space arises for the 'Golden Ticket' to take place, Lowe and ANU carve out a deeply personal and memorable experience for the audience member who finds themselves invited to participate in this interaction.

The level of creative vision that results from the synergies between Lowe and her co-artistic director Boss, a visual artist by training, may complicate further singular suggestions of authorship when reflecting on performances in their holistic shape. Indeed, this Element is acutely aware of the complexities in presenting *The Theatre of Louise Lowe* as a creative endeavour she pursues in isolation as it is precisely due to her particularly potent abilities for interconnection and collaboration that has resulted in her standing as a unique artistic visionary of the twenty-first century. She also leads the casting process for her productions, and in recent years, she has worked as a TV and film director and screenwriter in Ireland (ANU, Abbey Theatre, Gate Theatre, Landmark Productions, RTÉ, Screen Ireland) while her live performance work is increasingly commissioned internationally (LIFT *These Rooms* 2018; BAM-commission *The Cholera Season* in 2019, cancelled due to COVID) as her reputation gathers momentum. There is no doubt that Lowe is a playwright in addition to a director; however, this study is hesitant to conclude that Lowe is any singular title such as 'director' or 'playwright' in isolation, as the last decade has shown how swiftly her skillset extends and reforms, often in response to the cultural, social, and political conditions informing the arts sector more widely.

Throughout two decades of creative practice, Lowe's theatrical loyalties have remained rooted in the struggling working class of Dublin's city centre. Crowe praises her ability to absorb Irish events and histories considered too traumatic to be addressed comprehensively in political and cultural circles, while suggesting a concern for what impact this may take on Lowe, or indeed artists more generally, who regularly delve into the most troubling parts of social history. Lowe's experience of poverty marked her childhood and her access to theatre and the arts in ways that continue to inform her work. Indeed, how does one reconcile the vying issues of modest representations of class and poverty in Ireland (Pierse, 2017, 2020) alongside potential exclusion of those very communities from attending theatre due to ticket prices? It is worth qualifying this issue to suggest that any such exclusions are unintentional as the wider economic contexts for theatre production are so financially precarious that to remove or reduce ticket prices could mean production is no longer viable. Regardless, the fact remains that the cost of the ticket is a discretionary expense for most people, and communities that suffer economic hardship on a regular basis do not possess discretionary funds. Lowe's work, predominantly produced as part of ANU Productions, begins from the premise that they make work with communities, not about them (Lowe and Boss, 2023). 'Production' is not a fitting bandwidth for what they do (Lowe and Boss, 2023) as seeking dramaturgical satisfaction in any conventional sense of beginning-middle-end stories, with a central conflict resolved within 90 minutes, is a fool's errand, or, perhaps, a theatre critic's one.

This Element opens with this snapshot of Lowe's early years to understand the depth of Othering her experience of poverty resulted in, and, indeed, the bonds of kinship that she became nourished by from her tight-knit community in similar circumstances. Born in Foley Street in Dublin's north inner city in 1974, Lowe is loyal to presenting stories of vulnerable communities, particularly those areas that suffer economic deprivation and the legacies that arise from it. In her youth, Lowe regularly visited Dublin's Hugh Lane Gallery. There was (and remains) no entrance fee to the national art galleries and museums in Ireland, though certain special collections may require costed or timed tickets. Lowe became drawn to Renoir's *Les Parapluies* (*The Umbrellas*), a painting that foregrounds a woman in working-class attire, exposed to the elements without the shelter of a hat or umbrella in contrast to those surrounding her. Her expression is difficult to read, but amidst the jostling crowd, a sense of isolation emanates. Lowe's connection to this image is telling; it speaks to the hierarchies that dominate public space. Raised in a community ravaged by Ireland's first heroin epidemic in the 1970s (RTÉ Archives, 1972), these childhood experiences marked how she perceives community, equality, and political systems. The visit to this gallery became followed by visits to other galleries, and eventually theatre, as a sense of personal connection to artistic environments began to develop. Lowe understands the transformational potential that art can offer any individual, claiming 'theatre saved me' (2023). It is difficult to challenge her insights into the development of her own artistic abilities, but I would suggest that rather than 'saving' her, theatre tapped into abilities she already possessed, perhaps providing her with the confidence and conditions for those abilities to thrive. Introducing *The Theatre of Louise Lowe* must begin with this consideration of economic deprivation as a formative experience, but there are other significant strands of artistic experience that constitute her motivations and desires for the work she makes. The impact of growing up in Dublin's inner city has taught her the importance of community and of enabling communities to speak with their own voice rather than being spoken for.

1.2 Lowe, Owen Boss, and ANU Productions

Lowe and Boss first met while undertaking a postgraduate certificate in Youth Arts in the academic year of 2004–05, awarded through Maynooth University with the National Youth Council of Ireland. They both recall that they fell out spectacularly on their first day during a heated conversation regarding what may constitute art (Lowe and Boss, 2021). For Boss, it could be anything: no limits, no borders, no rules. For Lowe, intention and skill were fundamental ingredients for an activity, encounter, or object to earn the title 'art'. Despite a testy start, they became good friends during their programme which examined how to work with young people outside of mainstream education through art (Boss, 2024). At the time, Boss reflects how nervous and shy he was, while Lowe was Artistic Director of Roundabout Youth Theatre in Ballymun, a northern suburb of Dublin developed in the 1960s to accommodate social housing during a national housing crisis. The impact of working in Ballymun and the history of Ballymun carry significant weight in terms of the Lowe-Boss collaborative journey and the formation of ANU more widely, as it encapsulates some of the founding elements of ANU's blueprint for developing work. This blueprint includes foregrounding community-led concerns, marginalised groups and individuals, complex social histories, and patching together an alternative modern history of the island of Ireland from the voices and perspectives of those born and raised in some of Ireland's most vulnerable communities.

Lowe and Boss's first co-production took place in Ballymun with Lowe's youth theatre group from that area. For background, some of Dublin's inner-city communities were relocated to Ballymun before the newly developed residential area had sufficient civic infrastructure in place to support its residents. The area became synonymous with a boisterous community spirit in addition to major social challenges. The 'Ballymun flats', high-rise tower buildings that were new to Dublin's architecture, became visually symbolic of Ireland's struggling economy from the 1960s to the early 1990s in Dublin, before the Celtic Tiger economy propelled newer imagery associated with the speedy rise of the urban middle class, a phenomenon occurring much later in Ireland than in European counterparts. As Irish author and journalist Fintan O'Toole details, Dublin Corporation initially considered what became known as the Ballymun flats as 'system-building experiments' (O'Toole, 2016). According to O'Toole, the motivations for this type of residential construction were steeped in a political ideology that was bordering on desperation to enter modernity in the same vein as London, Paris, and other European capitals. As he recalls of the time, 'Ireland was sick of being a rural idyll of underdevelopment and mass emigration ... Hard as it is to reconcile with the later history of the place, Ballymun was part of the new optimism' (2016).

Widely documented in the decades since the construction of the Ballymun flats, those required amenities did not materialise. Sufficient public transport links between the area and the city centre were not in place. Ballymun became culturally associated with the concept of no man's land, reserved for the most economically and socially vulnerable, out of sight from the centre. O'Toole summarises both the civic and the psychological space of Ballymun following decades of poor planning, insufficient investment, and fundamentally, a lack of care by the political mainstream:

> By the mid-1980s traditional families were already reluctant to settle in Ballymun and the tower blocks were disproportionately occupied by single mothers and their children, by single men (many recently moved from institutional care) and by people who had been homeless. Few of them had access to the income, jobs, services, and supports they needed. And because they were often politically disempowered the authorities did not feel pressure to maintain the blocks to a decent standard (2016).

Lowe understood the experience of growing up in a community disavowed by the centre. By 2004, the first of the towers were demolished and by 2015, all were gone. Their homes and community spaces, problematic as they were, were literally bulldozed into oblivion before their eyes. Ballymun's young people became the ensemble that formed Lowe and Boss's first production, *Tumbledowntown* (2005).

The impetus for this first collaboration between Lowe and Boss was a practical one, with both required to complete a practice project for their coursework. Boss had no experience working with young people, but Lowe invited him to collaborate with her ensemble as part of Roundabout Theatre. While Boss's background was fine art, he recognised their synergies during their course. One task they were required to complete as part of their studies was to distil their thinking and practice regarding working with young people into three words. For Lowe and Boss, two of their three words matched: autonomy and quality. These priorities set the tone for how they make work together. They successfully applied for public funding through a scheme called 'Breaking Ground', and Boss recalls, 'That wouldn't have come from me, that was Louise's motivation and determination' (2024). Boss reflects on

Tumbledowntown's artistic process as the seeds of what ANU became driven by in future years:

> [...] taking over an abandoned flat in Ballymun, working with 26 people of the youth theatre over the course of a summer, working through visual art, through theatre and sound, and looking at this general theme of past, present and future in Ballymun and what it meant to them. So that was basically the core idea ... and I think that became the blueprint of what ANU would become ... (Boss, 2024)

Lowe and Boss considered their youth group 'experts' as it was their experience and local knowledge that was fundamental to the creation of a narrative and aesthetic experience. Boss also recalls that Lowe's earlier work with the group rendered the entire production possible, explaining, 'even to get young people from that area to stand in a room and actually engage with art is a win' (Boss). Without her laying the foundations with the young people, ranging in age from approximately 14 to 18, Boss doubts that they could have completed the project.

This 'blueprint' included other key fixtures that would appear regularly throughout the next twenty years of work. First and foremost, Lowe and Boss work from the premise that they make work with communities, not about them. They are particularly interested in working-class histories, oral histories, and histories of those who have been disavowed by canonical narratives established throughout the twentieth century, often inextricably linked from a nationalist desire to set ideological parameters regarding the priorities and identity of the Irish nationhood project. They were and remain interested in different artforms and exploring the potential for cross-pollination, working off site or in very loaded sites for approximately 4–8 weeks, depending on the availability of casts, crew, and resources in general. Over time, they could see the cultivation of familial dynamic, one which fostered a clear sense of purpose regarding the distinct significance of each production and its impact in revealing historical narratives and experiences previously sidelined, suppressed, or overlooked. Many of the cast return again and again, but Lowe and Boss ensure that with each new production they 'blood new people' (Boss, 2024). They invest in the process, and everyone's voice matters in rehearsal while constructing scenes and encounters. Boss summarises Lowe's role in the creation of this ethos and working environment, stating, 'I think people would run through a brick wall for Louise, she has that capacity, she has that almost leadership role, like people say that about football managers, "I'd run through a brick wall for them"' (2024).

This commitment to community is most transparently captured in Lowe's and ANU's process and how they situate their audiences at the centre of the work. 'Co-presence' as leading ANU scholar Brian Singleton posits in *ANU*

Productions: The Monto Cycle (2016) is an essential strategy that she incorporates in her work, intensely visceral in *Laundry* whereby audiences were challenged 'at moments of committal and escape from the asylum/laundry [...] as well as to assist, interact and bear witness' (Singleton, p. 2). Indeed, her strong sense of belonging to a community also underpins the formation of the ANU ensemble with whom she makes the majority of her work. ANU offers a shared vision of art, creativity, and innovation in terms of form, style and intention, but it also offers Lowe community, belonging, and a sense of support in making the work as she envisions it, which rarely corresponds to a singular artistic discipline, but pushes at the intersecting boundaries of 'performance, installation, visual art, choreography, site-responsive and community arts' (Singleton, p. 1).

These formative and artistic influences deeply inform her motivation to reframe audience experiences in Ireland. Lowe's core philosophy regarding the intersection of performance and audience that 'It should matter that you are there' (Lowe, 2013a) implicitly challenges the convention of much standard modern theatre in Ireland comprising end-on staging with audiences in darkness and a hefty fourth wall keeping that distance. In this style of staging work, how much does it matter if the audience is there? Engaging new audiences, capturing and keeping audience attention, generating inspiration, and activating critical engagement can be sought, but again, at a polite distance. However, the removal of live audiences from the performance space during COVID-19 lockdowns underlined the significance of audience presence and that without those bodies, elements of the very fundamental experience that constitutes the theatrical event changes. Some artists and critics will argue this is an existential threat, while others will advocate for the inclusion of virtual and hybrid technologies as part of innovation and shifts in practice in cultural spaces and production techniques.

Lowe's dramaturgy is dependent on harnessing the vitality of live audience presence by removing those conditions that allow for polite distance, and simultaneously, revealing a potential for violence within these social codes of politeness. This type of audience contract, one of 'polite distance', aligns with a wider social contract, also 'polite distance'. To say that Lowe reconfigures or indeed reimagines 'polite distance' is akin to equating the climate emergency with some weather issues. It is not that her practice bypasses theatre conventions, but, rather, reinvigorates them appropriate to the conditions of twenty-first-century experience to enable intimate connections that contemporary neoliberal social structures often prevent. As Kavanagh and Lowe detail:

> By placing the audience at the very centre of our practice in order to create autonomous exchanges, we have created a new kind of hybrid theatrical model of performance. Working in real environments and slippage between

the artificial and the real, we are interested in the changing nature of contemporary cultural thinking. We [...] use immersive engagement to create shared intimacies between audience and place and audience and performer. (p. 119)

For Lowe and ANU, performance-making is an act of enquiry conducted with communities that occurs through multidisciplinary research and becomes constructed by this 'Cubist dramaturgy', through which they do not present a singular perspective but confront multiple perspectives, drawing from varied artistic disciplines and strategies, and most often, without offering a resolution or conclusion.

The concept of Cubist dramaturgy as a guiding methodology did not stick immediately for Boss. His background in fine art immediately provoked ideas of 'the muse', typically female and not always well-treated, with the Cubist masters such as Pablo Picasso (1881–1973) in particular, and Georges Braque (1882–1963). He felt the association with Cubism and the modernist idea of the male painter/genius did not fit with the work ANU wanted to make or how they wanted to make it. With time however, he has found that it can be a helpful way to explain their process of looking at ideas, people, and histories from different angles. Boss brings this background in fine art with all its loaded resonance to the work ANU makes, just as Lowe brings her particular abilities in writing, directing, and casting. Interestingly, until Boss worked with Lowe on the Ballymun project, he had not been to see theatre, with the exception of the pantomime as a child. Thus, the set design and scenographic experiences he curates with Lowe for ANU are not an explicit intention to reject the traditions of naturalistic kitchen-sink dramas or pastoral quality (PQ) so resonant of twentieth-century Irish drama. Rather, he is inspired more acutely by smells, sounds, and sites. Like the work itself, Boss explains 'its multilayered and diverse across profession, across viewpoints, across age and to have that diversity gives us different ways of looking and responding' (2024).

Singleton summarises the impact of ANU's breakthrough performances known as 'The Monto Cycle' in his book of the same name. He maintains that ' ... no one is able to capture the complexity and multiplicity of performative strategies used by ANU Productions to enable spectators to encounter the history, people, geography and very materiality of the Monto' (2016, p. 3). He identifies the driving focus of ANU's work directed by Lowe as 'on 'others', the bystanders to history, on those absent from historical constructions. But in their folding of the present into the performed past, a folding the company calls 'NOW-THEN-NOW', new 'others' emerge as bystanders, inviting us to stand by them as well' (2021, p. 302). His research unveils the particular potency this dramaturgical motivation offers for Ireland's intercultural and multicultural communities, platforming the diversity of Irish communities, no easy task in a nation psychologically entrenched with a monolithic narrative of nationalism characterised as white, patriarchal, Catholic, heterosexual, and rural. He details:

> This otherness of ANU Productions is not strictly intercultural at first glance as most of their work in Ireland has been based on both state archives but also oral histories of communities through times of postcolonial revisionism, social deprivation and historical erasure. But it becomes intercultural, as we shall see, in moments in performance when visuality and aurality take a turn away from a monocultural past to perform in the present. (pp. 302–3)

While Singleton provides a granular focus on the intercultural threads of Ireland's past and present as captured through ANU's work, this study will provide a direct focus on Lowe's methods of practice which 'unfold' (Schneider, 1997, p. 2) the female body in moments of intense hardship, revealing the inheritance of church-state rule conjoined in a patriarchal capitalist nexus that continues to bear influence in state, civic, and community relations in the twenty-first century. Reading from Diana Taylor's *The Archive and the Repertoire*, geographer Karen Till analyses the 'body memory' performed in *These Rooms* (ANU and CoisCéim co-production, 2016 Dublin, 2018 London) directed by Lowe. Noting that each movement has been built upon a 'why' Till summarises, 'The artists critically interrogated the truth claims and silences of official institutions through creating more inclusive 'archives of public culture', whereby 'possible scenarios of alternative kinds of social relations' were made accessible to diverse audiences' (2018, p. 37). This method of performance research is framed by Lowe's directorial parameters as Till examines, noting Lowe's first response to archival materials pertaining to the 1916 North King St Massacre in Dublin was the following question: 'What was the experience of female bodies in these spaces?' (p. 37). This thread will be interrogated further in my close reading of *The Wakefires* (2022) co-produced with Cork Midsummer Festival and *Hammam* (2023–4) co-produced with the Abbey Theatre in Section 3 of this Element. During these productions, I shadowed Lowe during rehearsals as she juggled history, narrative, performance, design, technical demands, community responses, and, unfortunately for *The Wakefires*, the COVID-19 pandemic which ended the sold-out performance run following two previews attended by eight people.

As Lowe's theatre practice is largely produced by ANU with core members of the ensemble, much of this Element's focus is Lowe's work in that context. It is interesting to note that Lowe registered the name 'ANU' in 2009, which colloquially refers to a 'Goddess of Wealth' though stemming from the Celtic etymology of 'Ana', 'Anann', 'Dana' 'Danu' (MacKillop, 2004) with closer links to 'giver of life'. Celtic mythology refers to 'Anu' as 'The principal goddess of pre-Christian Ireland, the mother or "nourisher" of the Tuatha Dé Danann, the "people, tribe, or nation of Ana"' (MacKillop). In 2009, Ireland was bankrupt, bailed out by the European Commission (EC), the European Central Bank (ECB), and the International Monetary Fund (IMF), together comprising 'The Troika'. Economic crisis aside, the country was bankrupt culturally and socially, and arguably spiritually, following more than a decade of abuse revelations in Ireland's institutions and schools led by religious orders, often with state complicity and cover-ups on both sides of the border that separates Ireland from the north of Ireland (Clann Project; Historical Institutional Abuse Inquiry; Justice for Magdalenes Research; One in Four; Tuam Oral History Project). However, Lowe is not referring to economic wealth but something else, a force or energy that one must have within oneself and to connect with others to live with hope, dignity, and peace of mind. That primary reach for self-constitution and meaningful connection with others drives her vision for performance, identifying visual and embodied threads for 'ethical encounters' (Lowe qtd in Haughton 2014a, p. 73) between performers and audiences in places with charged and conflicting histories.

Certain dramaturgical threads emerge on analysis of her work since *The Monto Cycle* began in 2010. These include the impact of poverty and class discrimination on the development of society in Ireland, the political presentation of the female body in performance contexts, the trials and tragedies of mothers as a result of capitalist, patriarchal and religious control, and the reliance on mothers for assurance of familial and community survival. However, her productions often implicitly signal that 'mothering' extends far beyond the literal circumstances of birth. If not 'giver of life' as the Celtic etymology of 'Anu' suggests, certainly a 'nurturer' or 'sustenance' of life becomes a point of emotional significance visible in much of her work. Finally, a sense of communion as connection with others in the immediate present as well as connection with historical legacies is paramount in how she crafts performance encounters. While analysis of text to context is the shorthand for critique of drama in traditional academic models, for this Element, it is analysis of Lowe's practice to Lowe's place, north inner-city Dublin, that offers the most direct and useful lens for critique.

By 2015, Lowe's reputation for staging the experiences of Ireland's vulnerable communities, particularly those in poverty, was established with each of ANU's productions sold out, often in a matter of minutes. She expressed no interest in bringing to life the historical experiences of 'posh boys' according to Lar Joye, the then-Curator of Irish Military History at the National Museum of Ireland (NMI) in Collins Barracks in 2015 (Joye, 2024). This history concerns

Figure 2 *PALS – The Irish at Gallipoli* (2015). Performer Liam Heslin,
Image by Pat Redmond.

the final days of a young battalion of Irishmen before they left for the battlefields of Gallipoli in 1915, most never to return, the subject matter at the centre of ANU's *Pals – the Irish at Gallipoli* (2015) (Figure 2) directed by Lowe, supported by the NMI and the Department of Arts, Heritage and Gaeltacht in association with the National Archives of Ireland.

Joye contextualises how the concept of 'Pals' emerged in the British army, 'Armies rely on innocent under-25-year-olds rushing off to war because the generals don't do the fighting. So you need young, enthusiastic men to do your fighting for you. The idea was that people from the same clubs or associations would all join up as one unit (Joye qtd in Wallace, *Irish Times*, 2015). Journalist Arminta Wallace contextualises how the level of present-day knowledge concerning Irish involvement in Gallipoli is modest within Irish communities, with little enthusiasm displayed for bridging that gap prior to the centenary commemorations. However, Joye found stories and images of the Irish battalion captured in the 1917 book *The Pals of Suvla Bay*, the 'record of 'D' Company, 7th Royal Dublin Fusiliers, at Gallipoli' (Royal Dublin Fusiliers). It is these first-hand accounts that convinced Lowe and ANU to create their work staged at the NMI. Through their research, they discovered a variety of Irish men from different backgrounds and faith sent to Gallipoli as part of the British army. The tragedy of this story is not only the intense loss of young life, but the innocence possessed by these young men believing they stood a chance against the enemy, when in reality, 'five guys with a machine gun could stop 700. That was the horror of the new warfare' (Joye qtd in *Irish Times*). Joye wanted to showcase the histories of that battalion as it demonstrates the reality that 'when you're 18 you can't pick your enemy ... if you don't follow military law you get shot. I hate this jingoistic approach to war, 'joining an army is a noble, gentlemanly pursuit'. Its not: its dirty, its violent and its brutal' (2024).

Lowe and ANU's close working ties with Joye were cemented through that production, and their impact on public engagement with the Museum audiences notable. As a result of *Pals*, the museum experienced '9,000 visitors seeing the 300 performances and increasing the museum's visitor attendance by 34%' (Joye and Lowe, 2015, p. 137). That relationship developed into future work, including *On Corporation Street* (2016) in Manchester, England co-produced with HOME Manchester, and *The Book of Names* (2021) co-produced with Landmark Productions staged at Dublin Port, where Joye is currently Port Heritage Director. Joye had initially heard of ANU's work through *Living the Lockout* (2013), inviting them to screen a recorded version at the NMI. At the time, Joye reflects 'Louise was the only one doing anything exciting about the centenary ... Louise, Owen and the ANU gang are the few people who tackled the centenary properly' (Joye, 2024). Joye confided his feelings of dismay to Crowe regarding the inadequate resources to produce an NMI DoC programme that could achieve anything other than a 'tokenistic' encounter. Crowe pushed him to consider what would communicate Ireland's complex histories in such a way so as 'to shake people to their core and upset them and concern them' (qtd in Joye, 2024). He felt 1916 [the Easter Rising] was going to be 'done to death' and wanted to illuminate other significant events that were less known, yet equally profound in their significance to communities in Ireland and among the Irish diaspora, estimated at 70 million in 2017 (Gilmartin and Murphy, 2024). With ANU, Joye saw the potency of the NMI's objects and artefacts reinvigorated with new energy and opportunities to make meaningful connections with the public. He reflects the museum's relationship with ANU was a relatively new departure for them at the time, and they 'threw stuff at her [Lowe] for months ... She took it all on ... her people skills, her leadership skills are some of the best I've ever encountered' (2024). Part of these interpersonal and leadership skills include listening and learning as a primary point of departure, which operated as a key research phase for *On Corporation Street* (2016) (Figure 3) in Manchester city, commemorating the 20-year anniversary of the IRA bomb, the largest bomb to explode in the UK since WWII (BBC, 2022). Prior to rehearsals, ANU conducted three major inquiries with communities in Manchester who experienced the bomb and its aftermath to gather testimony. Of this process, ANU acknowledges that 'we were not the experts on the bomb and its effect but needed to form an archive from which to create the work. We needed to listen to the voice of the city and this repository of information was

Figure 3 *On Corporation Street* (2016). Performer Niamh McCann, Image by Pat Redmond.

instrumental in shaping, developing and making *On Corporation Street'* (ANU *Inquiries: On Corporation Street* 2016).

Both Joye and Crowe led focus groups in Manchester to gain a first-hand understanding of local memories. It was during this time that Joye felt history shake him 'to his core', rather than intending such an impact on audiences. While listening to individuals recount their memories of the bomb, it became clear that this was the first time many of those people were asked or interviewed about it in any formal capacity. While the IRA bomb wreaked havoc and injured more than 250 people, it did not kill (BBC). As there were no fatalities, the level of trauma associated with the bomb's impact seems to be minimised in public discourse and political action (Joye, 2024). Listening to these oral histories, memories, and reflections gave greater credence to those experiences. They were the voices that had been overlooked despite the atrocity they suffered. If there is any meaningful point to these centenary commemorations, Joye proposes, it is whether they change anything on their conclusion (2024). That remains to be seen with the official centenary commemorations ending in 2023, and this Element going to press in 2025. However, Lowe's role in the psychology of this public space is significant, particularly in staging the absent voice and body, 'unfolding' it as Rebecca Schneider suggests, 'Peeling at signification, bringing ghosts to visibility' (1997, p. 2).

1.3 Element Overview

This Element will offer micro and macro analyses of productions directed and sometimes written by Lowe since the conclusion of her first major theatrical intervention, the four-part 'Monto Cycle' (ANU, 2010–2014) as already mentioned. Following this work, I argue there is a greater confidence and determination in Lowe's creative voice and strategies, built upon the resilience harnessed as a result of the Monto Cycle's impact. Inherent in what follows is Lowe's deconstruction of gendered and classed lines in Irish social life primarily, epitomised by the character of Nannie in *The Lost O'Casey* (ANU, 2018) (Figure 4), a performance crafted in response to Irish playwright Seán O'Casey's *Nannie's Night Out* (1924). Nannie becomes a type of 'Everywoman' or 'Every-protagonist' for Lowe, operating not as 'real' representation of a particular individual but suggestive of an intergenerational encapsulation of struggling communities born into deprivation, overwhelmed by their circumstances, ostracised by the social fabric and let down by the political establishment. While O'Casey's 'Nannie' is developed from a 'real' woman he observed, 'Mild Millie' (*Drums under the Windows*, 1945), Lowe's various Nannies capture the 'why' of the struggle, and how her struggles for change are inextricably linked to place. If community conditions were tended to, restorying might emerge.

Figure 4 *The Lost O'Casey* (2018). Performer Sarah Morris, Image by Pat Redmond.

Leading the analysis in various case studies throughout this Element is Rebecca Schneider's theorisation of feminist motivations and intentions in contemporary performance art in *The Explicit Body in Performance* (1997), which addresses the conditions faced by women artists accessing key venues for the presentation of their work beginning in the 1980s in the United States. She recalls 'The Guerrilla Girls' posters in New York from 1985 onwards, with one such poster asking the public 'DO WOMEN HAVE TO BE NAKED TO GET INTO THE MET MUSEUM?' (p. 1). This question pithily summarises centuries of women's experience in patriarchal societies: in short, that how women are presented and represented in arts and culture is a battleground. The Guerrilla Girls refer to their strategy of intersectional feminism to undermine 'the idea of a mainstream narrative by revealing the understory, the subtext, the overlooked, and the down-right unfair' (Guerilla Girls). Most often, it is images of women that please the gaze of the white heterosexual male for capitalist ends of endless circulation, reproduction, and profit that are regularly included, and these images do not resonate with the majority of women's lives. Lowe presents women who do not please the gaze of heterosexual white men in neoliberal culture but who have suffered as a result of the demands, expectations and priorities of that gaze, such as how it constructs and embeds conditions of desire, power, and privilege. Schneider notes how the very name of the group refers to both gender and race that are accorded lesser status in social relations, while the masks they use 'make explicit a social contract' (p. 1). To render visible this social contract, these feminist performance artists utilised a strategy of 'explosive literality' (p. 2) through their art and actions. Lowe, and much of ANU's body of work, also stage a type of 'explosive literality' that keenly questions assumptions of the social contract that appear invisible and unspoken, and yet could not be more explicit in terms of which community benefits and suffers, as Dublin GP Dr Austin O'Carroll emphasises in his developmental work for *The Lost O'Casey*.

O'Carroll works from an inner-city medical practice and became centrally involved in ANU's 'community encounters' as part of their intense develop-ment period for *The Lost O'Casey* (*TLOC*) in 2018, written and directed by Lowe, staged at the invitation of the north inner-city community where she was raised. However, O'Carroll's collaborations with Lowe stretch back further than *TLOC*, outlined further in Section 2. From his programme note, he details the frustration of seeing how the cards are stacked against north inner-city commu-nities and such conditions become embedded and structural. Dr O'Carroll criticises the social and political conditions which result in:

> [...] families who have lost several children to drug addiction, young
> parents and children in homelessness, young intelligent adults leaving

school after their junior cert, migrant families living year on impotent year in asylum-seeker purgotary [. . .] And then, the ultimate injustice, that same community is blamed for it's own misfortune. Slothful social welfare scammers, worthless junkies, contemptible alcoholics etc. (O'Carroll, *TLOC* in DTF Programme 2018)

TLOC will be further analysed in Section 2, yet O'Carroll's insights are central to introducing how and why Lowe and ANU conceive of and frame their productions, performed in the streets and spaces of communities to the wonder, delight, and, indeed, discomfort of audiences and passers-by.

'Explicit' captures the central objective of Schneider's study as she evokes its Latin roots 'explicare' meaning 'to unfold'. From here, Schneider's concept of 'unfolding the body' emerges, a concept which frames the analysis of Lowe's work throughout this Element:

Unfolding the body, as if pulling back velvet curtains to expose a stage, the performance artists in this book peel back layers of signification that surround their bodies like ghosts at a grave. Peeling at signification, bringing ghosts to visibility, they are interested to expose not an originary, true, or redemptive body, but the sedimented layers of signification themselves. (p. 2)

Unfolding the body is a powerful lens through which to critique Lowe's work. Recent productions directly stage documentary materials relating to Ireland's Decade of Centenaries (2012–2023) which commemorate, but by no means celebrate, 100 years since the partition of the Island of Ireland into two states, the 26-county Irish state and 6-county Northern Irish state, following major wars with the British Empire and Irish Civil War (Ferriter, 2022; 2015). In these productions, there is no 'true or redemptive body' (Schneider, p. 2). Rather, Lowe provokes those 'sedimented layers of signification' (p. 2) to become fertile and active soil for contemporary reflection and debate. 'Bringing ghosts to visibility' (p. 2) is a poignant encounter in the context of the centenary commemorations, where figures such as 'Nannie' re-emerge from archival records, telling us their stories which did not find solace in any conventional resolution symptomatic of a functioning society.

To conclude this section, I summarise essential ingredients for Lowe's work which will re-emerge for fresh analysis within close readings of distinct performances throughout this Element. These ingredients include that Lowe's productions are often directly immersed in a historical stimulus, though she approaches each production as a unique and distinct encounter without a predefined outcome. She does not stage the past as it has been written or disregarded, but excavates the past to reassess and re-present ideas, legacies, absences, and questions. Lowe restorys these stimuli, contextualising them in the historical period of their occurrence and simultaneously in the contemporary moment of performance, which produces a space of self-reflection for audiences, seeing themselves as part of a social journey. Her creative team will include core members of the ANU ensemble, but will also directly involve anthropologists, architects, archivists, folklorists, historians, medics, and social scientists. Indeed, some have been interviewed as part of this study's research methodology. Within this network of materials and expertise that she gathers with her ensemble, who become 'dramaturgs of their own work' (Lowe, 2012), Lowe stages a historically situated chain of events revealed through multiple protagonists and spaces of performance that compel, unsettle, complicate, and, most significantly within her work, remain unresolved.

2 Staging Ireland's Nannies

2.1 Lowe's Dublin

'Will you let me alone, will you leave me for this?' (Irish Street Medicine Symposium: https://www.drugs.ie/multimedia/video/international_street_medi cine_symposium_2014). These are the words recalled by Dublin inner-city GP Dr Austin O'Carroll of a female patient in recovery from heroin addiction performing an autobiographical encounter from her past. O'Carroll sought Lowe's collaboration as part of the International Street Medicine Symposium hosted by Safetynet in Dublin in 2014 (ISMS SafetyNet). Working with two of his patients, she paired them with performers and tasked them to rewrite part of their own stories. The final scenes were performed for the conference delegates, including this woman with a history of heroin addiction. The woman and the performer she worked with took their audience down an alleyway where she had frequently injected. One Christmas evening however, following 'tapping' (begging for money), she realised she was alone in the world. She went to this alleyway, injected, and then was approached by a young Garda (Irish language, 'police'). She pleaded with the Garda for her solitude so that she could escape into the alternate reality the heroin provided. After a brief moment's hesitation, the Garda turned around and walked away.

This image is both distressing and provocative. It demonstrates how abject experiences may circulate socially, including in official relations such as engagement from authorities. Thinking of 'Nannie' from *The Lost O'Casey* as a type of 'Everywoman' for Lowe's work as an embodiment of intergenerational discord in Irish society, introduced in Section 1, one can see how the pull of social alienation manifests in this scene between the woman and the Garda. Both the woman and the Garda know the Garda should intervene officially, and yet, neither personally desire the intervention. Julie Kristeva considers how strange and discomforting the affect of abjection manifests in western cultural experience:

> This massive and abrupt irruption of a strangeness which, if it was familiar to me in an opaque and forgotten life, now importunes me as radically separated and repugnant. Not me. Not that. But not nothing either. A whole lot of nonsense which has nothing insignificant, and which crushes me. At the border of inexistence and hallucination, of a reality which, if I recognise it, annihilates me. Here the abject and abjection are my safety railings. Seeds of my culture (p. 126).

Lowe stages these seeds and invites her audience to remove the 'radical separate[d] and repugnant' relation into the space one typically inhabits. In order to preserve middle-class codes embedded in the social fabric – stable, comfortable and respectable – scenes of despair, bodily chaos, and social exclusion must be kept in dark alleyways, away from the centre. Did the Garda in that instance uphold unwritten social codes that one may internalise over time or abandon their duty? What do concepts of duty and society really mean when so many are enabled to exist outside of a functioning public sphere?

The image of this woman alone in an inner-city alleyway on Christmas Eve injecting heroin while begging a Garda to turn away returns this analysis to Schneider's 'unfolding of the body' (p. 2) as part of Lowe's heightened realistic aesthetic which render visible the scars on the wounded bodies from the past that Lowe revives for the present. Authorities turning away from those most vulnerable is not a new narrative in Irish theatre, as Seán O'Casey reveals in his 1945 autobiography *Drums under the Windows*. 'Mild Millie' is a woman he meets by chance one day as minds his sister's furniture on the street, who has been recently evicted from her residence along with her children. O'Casey is waiting for a cart to arrive to collect the furniture when he sees Mild Millie. Drunk from methylated spirits, Mild Millie challenges a passing police constable and a sergeant to acknowledge her, as O'Casey describes in the story 'Behold, My Family is Poor'. The constable advises the sergeant to 'Take no notice of her . . . it's Mild Millie – a terrible female, powerful woman, takin' ten men to lug her to the station when she goes wild with red biddy; take no notice, for God's sake' (O'Casey, 1945, p. 80). O'Casey reflects on how the encounter came to a conclusion, with Millie declaring, 'It's you, you ignorant yucks, that breed th' throuble; g'on now, she shouted after them, for they had turned and walked away as if they hadn't laid an eye on her or heard a word she said' (p. 80).

Returning to Lowe's work with the medical conference, O'Carroll later received correspondence from a medic in the United States who had been in attendance. Following a staunch refusal to provide methadone treatment to heroin addicts throughout his medical career, believing it served to replace one addiction with another, he began training to provide methadone to his patients (O'Carroll, 2023). The performance encounters staged as part of the conference illuminated a deeper and more holistic perspective of those battling addiction, leading to significant shifts in the medic's thinking and practice. In this case, Lowe's work brought the abject to the centre. By unfolding those bodies to the conference delegates, the psychological and cultural contexts that usually propel communities to avert their gaze to avoid connecting with scenes of discomfort and despair were halted. Instead, the performance crafted by Lowe directed their focus to those scenes in a visceral collective encounter.

O'Carroll has worked in Dublin's north inner city since 1991, treating the devastation caused by the widespread introduction of heroin in the 1980s to communities already disadvantaged by intergenerational conditions of poverty. He initially met Lowe in his capacity as her family's GP. He reflects on how social discourse refers to the omnipresence of narcotics in all communities but challenges the underlying generalisations that thinking may suggest. 'You've got cannabis and powder cocaine for well-off areas, but heroin and crack for the poor areas. More people die from drugs overdoses than road crashes in Ireland, but you wouldn't know that from media representation' (O'Carroll, 2023). O'Carroll brought trainee GPs to see ANU's *The Boys of Foley St* (2012) directed by Lowe as part of their training, as the production addressed the emergence, distribution and class politics of heroin in the local area from the 1970s (Haughton, 2014b; Singleton, 2016; Hill, 2017). He also gave talks to the ANU team on his experience of working locally for approximately three decades during their rehearsals for *The Lost O'Casey*, a performance that delivers close encounters with Dublin's inner-city communities through a handful of characters, as briefly touched upon in Section 1. Of his time working with Lowe through his medical practice and outreach, and through the development work for ANU's productions, he concludes, 'I think Lowe is like a witness, almost like a retrospective witness to this story that just didn't hit the main news. And it isn't just a story about the deaths, though that's a big part of it, it's the devastation that happened across the inner-city upon a background of poverty' (2023).

O'Carroll's confidence in Lowe's practice is rooted in his belief that she finds a way for theatre audiences to see, or 'confront' as Crowe maintains (2023), certain realities of everyday life in inner city communities that for a variety of complex reasons, tend to be overlooked, marginalised, or not popular within mainstream Irish social discourse and cultural representation. The association of poverty and struggle may trigger a deeply embedded postcolonial consciousness, whereby Irish society seemed to swiftly transform into a postmodern social and cultural condition in the 1990s, which brought as many challenges as opportunities. For most of the twentieth century, Ireland was considered 'the sick man of Europe' (O'Carroll, 2023). Economic opportunities afforded by multinational investment in certain sectors pushed the overall national economy out of this 'sick man' analogy by the late 1990s; however, these statistics are not proportionate to social demographics nationally. The economics gains impacted the few, not the many. O'Carroll examines how the majority of Irish society now consider 'the poor' through the lens of 'charity'. On the one hand, he surmises that some countries do not offer much scope for charity and consequently, it is better to have something than nothing. On the other hand, he argues that charity is not an accurate methodology for confronting ongoing structural inequality, and most problematically, it 'dehumanizes and blames people, says you're at fault, its your problem. It's well intentioned, but that's the thesis underneath it. She [Lowe] challenges that and brings a richness of inner-city life, the richness of their experience' (2023).

Lowe understands the various conditions that create poverty both as a result of her own childhood experiences and from her professional encounters. Her early career in theatre includes working with vulnerable women in the Women's Resource Centre established in 2003 in Ballymun, an outer suburb of north Dublin, previously examined in Section 1. Details of Lowe's theatre classes in the Centre demonstrate how in this pedagogical context performance became a safe space for creativity, expression, as well as the development of community and confidence among the women. These women had faced various and multiple challenges in their lives, including challenges pervasive in the communities in which they resided. Motherhood, without sufficient supports, and economic disadvantage often dominated their life experiences. Lowe recalls from another workshop in Dublin that she ran in the late 1990s that one woman asked her to review some games and activities with her after class, so that she could perform them again at home with her children (Lowe, 2020). Lowe was happy to assist. As time progressed, other women in the class confided that this woman lived alone and her children were under the care of social services. Lowe realised this was not of importance in their shared space (Lowe, 2020). Lowe continued to discuss games and activities she could use with her children in future conversations. Lowe stresses that in a context such as this what is important is helping that woman become the mother she wants to be, regardless of her immediate circumstances. The ability to talk, to tell, to share, and to imagine: Lowe understood that these were the skills and strategies women needed to survive.

While much of Lowe's practice is dedicated to unfolding marginalised bodies to tell their own stories, this study does not comfortably situate Lowe as part of a momentum captured by Dani Snyder Young in *Theatre of Good Intentions* (2013). Snyder Young's study examines a cohort of 'artists and scholars [who] operate from a fundamental, utopian desire for theatre to make *social change*' (p. 2). Lowe's theatre does not necessarily possess roots in utopian desire from the development and production work I have experienced. Her roots are points of injustice in specific historical events and figures which continue to impact the present moment. While there are parallels with Lowe and indeed ANU's work in some of the underlying principles of Applied Theatre as Snyder Young sets out, such as the '"subversive potential" to "threaten the status quo" (Lev-Aladgem, 2010: 13), or "make social structures, power relations, and individual habitus visible, and at the same time provide tools to facilitate change" (Osterlind, 2008: 71)' (p. 2), Lowe's practice relishes staging complexities and contradictions where possible. In so doing, her work questions whether any form of certainty regarding historical relationships and power structures can be identified, much less transformed.

Lowe continued this work as a drama facilitator in Dublin prisons Wheatfield and Mountjoy throughout the late 1990s, working for the pre- and post-release prison services supported by the Department of Justice, in addition to delivering workshops at various resource centres. Though the working environment could be tough and tense, Lowe recounts that 'my accent saved me. I wasn't a prison officer, and I wasn't a traditional type of teacher' (Lowe, 2024). Throughout these experiences, the fundamental elements of Lowe's dramaturgy become formed and cemented: a process-led approach, staging or 'unfolding' the body, and, the practice of care in developing work with communities, not about them. From this period, Lowe has the creative DNA for 'Nannie' in *The Lost O'Casey*, a fitting return of O'Casey's character, informed by his own context of childhood poverty and economic struggle. O'Casey put the stories of the struggling north inner-city centre stage at the Abbey Theatre a century before Lowe, yet between the emergence of Nannie in the O'Casey play *Nannie's Night Out* from 1924, and Lowe's Nannie from 2018, the state(s) of Ireland are socially, economically, politically, and cultur- ally transformed and incomparable. Regardless, Nannie remains. These seis- mic shifts include:

- The Dublin Lockout (1913)
- the Easter Rising (1916)
- the War of Independence (1919)
- the Civil War (1920–1921)

- the partition of Ireland into the 26-county Irish Free State and 6-county north of Ireland/Northern Irish state (1921–1922)
- the Republic of Ireland (1937–1939)
- the 'Troubles' in the north of Ireland (1968–1998)
- the 'Celtic Tiger' economic boom (1996–2007)
- the Citizenship Referendum (2004)
- the EU-IMF Bailout (2010)
- the Marriage Referendum legalising gay marriage (2015)
- the Repeal the 8th Referendum legalising termination of pregnancy (2018)

Nannie's world remains, her challenges remain, and her vulnerability remains. How can a country change so radically in terms of its political governance and civic infrastructure, ideological influence, economic fortune, social and cultural expression, and yet for some people, not change at all?

2.2 Lowe, Kavanagh, and Artistic Process: 'How Do You Catch a Dream?'

'It's like a poem that's written backwards, and then you read it by the end' (Kavanagh, 2024), Kavanagh reflects on Lowe's process in the rehearsal room. Kavanagh is a founding member of the ANU ensemble, meeting Lowe following the conclusion of the 2009 Dublin Fringe Festival in which they both had work programmed. Kavanagh's play *Black Bessie* is a one-woman show she wrote and performed in, telling the story of a nomadic sculpture woman who the audience are intended to 'find' and be with for a time, but ultimately leave her. Staged at Merrion Square Park, the park rangers told Kavanagh they find women like Black Bessie regularly. In Kavanagh's piece, this woman has been sculpted by forces of church and state in Ireland. She is no longer tethered to the infrastructure of mainstream society but instead keeps her body connected to grass, soil, and the expansiveness of outside spaces. *Black Bessie* is deeply informed by Kavanagh's training in fine art and sculpture from the National College of Art and Design (NCAD) in Dublin. Similar to Boss, her creative roots are in art disciplines initially, later applied to performance, and her methods for rehearsing her roles include sketching and drawing throughout the development period (*Wakefires* rehearsal notes, Haughton, 2022; *Hammam* rehearsal notes, Haughton, 2023). Further training in performance and playwriting connected her to the multifaceted shape that live performance can inhabit, with Kavanagh's particular focus dis-tilled to strategies of embodiment, aligning with core tenets of Lowe's practice. Her instincts for audience connection chime directly with Lowe's and those of Boss. For Kavanagh, 'communion with the audience' (2024) is paramount in how they conceive of and construct performance encounters.

Lowe had directed *Basin* for the 2009 Dublin Fringe festival, programmed at the same time as *Black Bessie*, and so neither artist managed to meet or see each other's work. *Basin* was Lowe's first production to utilise elements of her personal life rather than another individual's or community's. Exploring the space of Dublin's Blessington St. Basin reservoir which supplied water to the north city, it is also the place where her father was warden and where Lowe's family lived for a time. From this space of her childhood home, one can identify that Lowe was exposed to the layering of stories on place at a formative stage in her youth. Furthermore, this particular homeplace was a point of intersection between her private familial space, and the public space and civic requirements of Dublin city. Thus, one might conclude that space for Lowe is inherently a layering of experiences and legacies, and moreover, reflects a spectrum of personal and communal belonging. In creating *Basin*, Lowe was 'interested in the palimpsest of life that informs the "soul" of the reservoir' according to theatre critic Sara Keating (2009). Keating considers Lowe's emerging relationship with sites of performance at this time, suggesting 'Choosing to perform plays in cramped derelict flats or aboard moving buses, you could say that she relishes throwing the impossible her way' (2009). Through the experience of making *Basin*, Lowe unpacks ANU's process of critically analysing space and site-specificity to keenly distinguish their interpretation from other artists or companies who operate outside of traditional theatre spaces yet do not operate from a parallel departure point of engaging with layered histories embedded in the site of performance. Lowe reveals:

> So it's not just a case of reflecting my family's memories but everything else that we discovered: whether that's how the reservoir was built in the late 1700s to give water to the whole of Dublin, or that the Jameson Distillery was once located here, or that the gate lodge was a brothel, or that James Joyce wrote part of *Ulysses* on a bench in the park. And then there have been the experience of the locals, who have been looking at us for the last few weeks wondering what we were doing, and then offering their own histories and memories, appearing with photographs and their own stories for us; how each of them feel ownership of the space in a different way (Lowe qtd in Keating, 2009).

From this 2009 Dublin Fringe Festival programme, Kavanagh and Lowe are both centring their performance narratives and strategies on the physical environment of their home city, revealing how certain bodies, politics, and experiences are entangled in society's shifting relationships with those sites. Though neither had sufficient financial resources in 2009 to produce their work in a theatre building, established theatre buildings would not have suited their creative intentions regardless of whether further funding had materialised. Elements of postmodern and postdramatic thinking and strategies can also be identified through both works, as performance scholar Sara Jane Bails details, which address 'the limitations posed by linguistic structures and traditional narrative conventions that now seem[ed] outmoded [...] Theatre language, itself a field of knowledge production, could be made to express intensities and mood-states rather than service the development of character and linear plot on stage' (Bails, p. xix). Neither *Black Bessie* nor *Basin* serviced the development of character or linear plot on stage, but instead, staged encounters to enable audiences glimpse narratives of the city less well-known, unveiling the rich tapestry of connections between site, story, and performance, like a prologue to the 'NOW-THEN-NOW' approach ANU formalises not long after. 'NOW-THEN-NOW' became constituted as ANU's leading dramaturgy through conversation led by founding member and performer Robbie O'Connor. In development for *World End's Lane* (2010, 2011) set at the start of the twentieth century, ANU struggled with the period costume and the language of the time. They realised the creative blockage they were encountering was caused by the fixity in time, and that their characters and actions needed to journey with the audience between the past and present in a type of collision.

Boss, Kavanagh, Lowe, and O'Connor are ANU's founding members, and their meeting became realised through a development day organised by Dublin Fringe on conclusion of the 2009 Festival. This occurred at The Lab, a multi-disciplinary city centre arts space located near 'the Monto' where Lowe was raised and where ANU's first major cycle of work was staged (2010–2014; Singleton, 2016). Kavanagh walked into a room and saw the early seeds of ANU's Monto Cycle mapped out on four walls: (1) images from Debbie's family's Romany tradition: Debbie is Lowe's best friend from childhood, now married to Boss; (2) photos of Amanda Coogan's work: Coogan is an internationally acclaimed Irish performance artist, trained by and collaborator of Marina Abramović who mentored Lowe in the early stages of her career; (3) drawings of Irishman Frank Duff (1889–1980): a civil servant and founder of the Legion of Mary, a Catholic organisation involved in establishing Mother and Baby Institutions in Ireland; (4) the work of Emma O'Kane: leading Irish dance artist (1977–2021) and Robin Wilson, internationally acclaimed lighting designer. In this memory, Kavanagh connects the core ideas that inspired the aesthetic and social roots of ANU: (1) exploring the diversity of communities that make up contemporary Dublin; (2) working across artistic disciplines to see what possibilities arise, in particular, through visual and performance art, dance, installation and theatrical performance and (3) examining the impact of the founding ideas that informed the creation of a conservative Catholic Irish State almost a century ago, following an embittered civil war between pro- and anti-Treaty forces (Anglo-Irish Treaty 1921–1922), further examined in the case studies *The Wakefires* (2022) and *Hammam* (2023–2024). Lowe and Boss discussed their plans to undertake a 100-year history of 'the Monto' as one production, later becoming four interconnected productions, 'The Monto Cycle', richly analysed in Singleton's 2016 monograph of the same name. During this meeting Lowe tells Kavanagh, 'I'm not sure what its going to be', signalling an open approach that Kavanagh felt motivated by (2024).

'What was the language in the room', Kavanagh ponders regarding her own reflections of this time as they began to develop *World End's Lane*, the first iteration of the 'The Monto Cycle' premiered in Dublin Fringe Festival in 2010 and restaged in Dublin Theatre Festival in 2011, alongside ANU's second iteration, *Laundry* (2011). She recalls that they organically spoke a shared language regarding performance, aesthetic, and connection with audiences. This sense of artistic connection led them to a develop a shorthand in their rehearsal and development work, which Kavanagh asserts includes a sense of understanding where they are going, though not necessarily a language that can literally be captured or explained in words. 'How do you catch a dream'? (2024) she asks rhetorically. To provide a stronger sense of clarity of their shared energies and intentions in the work, she turns to the significance of the historical figures they foreground, beginning with Honour Bright in *World's End Lane*. Bright, like Nannie, epitomises the figures from that past that Lowe finds and revives for the present. *World End's Lane* explored the 'Monto' area, which housed 'almost 6,000 prostitutes [in the] largest and most prolific red-light district in Europe, up until it's dramatic closure in one night by one man (Frank Duff, founder of the Legion of Mary) on 12th March 1925' (*World End's Lane*, ANU). Lowe recognises the gaps in official history, using ANU's productions to return these figures to public consciousness, acutely showcasing their suffering and strength, the contexts in which they lived, how their existence challenge the status quo, and, indeed, how they were punished for this by those with access to more power and privilege, at times, with impunity.

Bright's real name was Lizzie O'Neill and she was found shot dead in the Wicklow mountains not far from Dublin where she worked, age twenty-five, in June 1925 (Blain, 2008; Delay, 2020). Her death caused widespread scandal for numerous reasons. Firstly, Bright worked as a prostitute in addition to working in Pyms clothing store, having moved from rural Ireland to Dublin city for employment. Furthermore, she was identified as conversing with or fighting with (depending on differing accounts of the time) physician Patrick Purcell and policeman Leo Dillon outside Dublin's posh Stephen's Green Hotel before entering a car and driving away with these men, at a time when cars were rare

(Delay, 2020). Bright's body was discovered the next day killed by a gunshot through the heart. As argued by historian Cara Delay, the specifics of Bright's work, life, and death caused scandal and intrigue not only as a result of the violence she suffered. Indeed, the conditions of her existence challenged the strict narratives enforced by autocratic authorities in power at that time. Delay observes that a schism was occurring in western discourse surrounding women's rights at the time because of WWI, resulting in the increased prevalence of women in the public sphere while men were at war (2020). She details:

> By their very movement, unmarried migrants like O'Neill rejected fixity and domesticity, troubling contemporary understandings of Irish womanhood. As Maria Luddy has shown, a public obsession with immorality in the 1920s and 1930s articulated that 'the real threat to chastity and sexual morality resided in the bodies of women' (2020).

Any such explicit challenge to the status quo was to be met with punishment, both swift and severe. A Galway bishop strongly encapsulates the tone and tenor of social codes at the time, advising men to 'keep their willful daughters in line: If your girls do not obey you, if they are not in at the hours appointed, lay the lash on their backs. That was the good old system, that should be the system today' (qtd in Delay, 2020).

Part of Lowe's approach to creating the performance narrative includes creation from one's own unique voice, according to Kavanagh. As she had over a decade of acting work behind her, in addition to her work in fine art and sculpture, Kavanagh was established in her own artistic process where 'failure' was not a descriptor and the work is open to constant metamorphosis (Kavanagh, 2024). Lowe and Boss shared these strategies, experimenting with audiences of one and developing their work using 'imagery of the hour' (Kavanagh). She explains, 'if I'm here [in performance] for 12 hours, that's a behaviour, an invitation I understand. The abstraction of the invitation rather than one parallel logical line of thinking is key [to creating the work]' (2024). To convey this to their audiences throughout durational performances typically running for 10–12 hours per day, Kavanagh describes the work as 'a layering of artwork' (2024). For *World End's Lane*, as audiences came into the space, they are met by a 360-degree performance which has an openness of structure and sensory design. In embodying Bright for performance Kavanagh asserts, 'The back of my head is as important as the front' (2024) in the unfolding of this Irish lineage of intergenerational female trauma through these intimate encounters.

In finding out who Bright was or may have been, certain 'quirks' associated with the ANU process also manifest clearly for the first time. These quirks tend to make themselves known particularly through the excavation of wronged women from the past. For example, while ANU were rehearsing the performance *World End's Lane*, featuring Bright, in the offices of Rough Magic Theatre Company in Dublin city centre, they discovered that same building was once home to Pyms store where Bright had worked. For context, Dublin may be considered a small city by European standards, yet it is a capital city with a population of approximately half a million people, so the coincidence is noteworthy. The links between this performance and Ireland's performance history continue in unexpected ways. According to allegations by Bright's granddaughter, she believed her murdered grandmother was the mother of W.B. Yeats's lovechild, and this fact was part of the conspiracy in her murder (Malekmian, 2023). The 'quirks' continued to emerge as the seeds of *Laundry* began to formulate.

While in rehearsals for *World End's Lane* in the Monto area, Lowe and Kavanagh sat in Kavanagh's car one night across from the former derelict Magdalene Laundry building on Seán McDermott Street where *Laundry* was staged one year later as the second iteration of the Monto Cycle. Vacant for over a decade, the building was officially managed by Dublin City Council, with no person or organisation allowed use it due to health and safety protocols. After some time sitting in the car, the pair observed an upstairs light turn on, visible through one of the windows (Kavanagh, 2024). During lengthy rehearsals for *Laundry* the following year in the cold building (overcoming many challenges in gaining permission to use the building), the heating came on (Kavanagh, 2024). While in the technical space of the chapel for *Laundry*, there were four walkie-talkies not in use at that moment. At the same time, they each turned on and the sound of babies crying could be heard, though understandably the more cynical mind would suggest the noise is interference (Lowe, 2024). While shadowing Lowe for *The Wakefires* in 2022 as part of the research process for this Element, I observed further quirks. En route to rehearsals in Cork, performer Kate Finnegan drove from Dublin. Not far from Cork city, her car broke down. The mechanic who brought her to the garage to fix her car was the grandson of the woman she was playing in the performance (Haughton rehearsal notes, 2022). These anecdotes lead to joviality in conversation among the ensemble, as they confirm that working in ANU provokes multiple connections among the past and present not explicitly identified previously. It extends further than the past and present, channelling through night and day. At a certain point in rehearsals, cast and crew will ask each other if they have started 'showdreaming' yet (Haughton rehearsal notes, 2022; 2024), a shorthand for referring to the content of the performance absorbing their thoughts, dreams, and habits. Kavanagh asserts that this is a regular part of the process, as:

> The alchemy is happening ... You start to hear this broken, fragmented language that goes around the table ... reminds me of something young, with children, the excitement of pure joy in making. Its big work, the muscles are big, the ask is big, the psychology is big ... the [ANU] petri-dish – it includes the dream body, activates the political body. (2024)

It is this 'dream body' and 'political body' that intersect in Lowe's work, utilising the intimacy of those small one-to-one encounters with audiences for the 'big ask'. It demonstrates that the past remains present, once these 'ethical encounters' (Lowe, 2012) and 'moments of communion' (Lowe, 2012) are invited between public and performance.

2.3 'Nannie's No Home ... ': Lowe and Rehoming Ireland's Ghosts

In 2018, *The Lost O'Casey* presented audiences with the character 'Nannie', a figure first staged in Irish playwright Seán O'Casey's *Nannie's Night Out* (1924). The original text is rumoured to have burned alongside the Abbey's original theatre building in the 1950s though Irish theatre scholar José Lanters charts the play's colourful journey from 'been given by O'Casey to Gabriel Fallon [...] Fallon eventually sent the manuscript onto Robert Hogan, whose edition of the play, published in 1962, was "a recension of four varying and incomplete versions – the original typescript and three Abbey typescripts – and two pages of added material"' (2021, p. 63). Nannie occupies a space of contradiction: she is lost according to rumour, burned to ashes in the flames of the national theatre, offering imagery rich in symbolism. Yet, she is not lost but very much present generations later and in various updated scripts, through reworkings of her character in future O'Casey plays (Ayling, 1962; Lanters, 2021), and ANU's reimagining of key elements in their 2018 production. Nannie produces feelings of abjection as theorised by Kristeva (1982) as her character is violent, dirty, unpredictable, vulgar, and poor. Yet, Kristeva's theorisation is originally considered in terms of the maternal body, and Nannie is not a mother, so therefore not necessarily abject in any strictly literal interpretation. However, Nannie is often symbolically conceived of in relation to nationalistic tropes of Mother Ireland and her various myths, and so partially aligns with Kristeva's idea of the abject. As much as one may wish to keep Nannie at a distance, particularly in ANU's production, that is not possible, as Nannie physically leads the audience around Dublin city centre, confusing them as to what type of character she is, with a personality that alters radically and quickly from charming wit to violent outbursts, and ultimately, vulnerable individual, captured in the video clip that remains on the Abbey Theatre website (https://www.abbeytheatre.ie/whats-on/the-lost-ocasey/). Ayling's analysis picks up on this shift in her persona drawing from observers at the time, a character trait faithfully carried through from O'Casey's Nannie to Lowe's Nannie:

> [...] we may note the radical changes of mood and tension in Nannie's character, which shock the audience by their violence and speed and yet never seem incongruous or distracting. There is comic vigour of language and invective, and yet an all pervading sense of pathos here that gives point to O'Casey's remark to Holloway (Nov 2. 1924) that 'there are too many Nannies in the city – they are tragic figures not to be laughed at.' (Ayling, p. 158)

Like witnessing a car crash, one does not intend to stare, but the gaze is inevitably pulled towards the scene of human devastation.

In O'Casey's text, Nannie is recently released from Mountjoy Prison, known colloquially and ironically as 'the Joy', the same prison where Lowe worked almost a century later. In *Drums under the Windows,* O'Casey describes meeting Millie in great detail. According to his memory, Mild Millie is 'A young woman, hatless, a jagged skirt just reaching to her knees, showing a pair of hardy, well-shaped legs, with feet thrust deeply into a man's pair of rusty rough leather, Blucher boots came unsteadily down the street. A dark green shawl dangled from her shoulders, and a scaly basket, holding one stale fish, was hooked over her left arm' (1945, p. 70). During this unexpected encounter, this attractive, but wild, woman, 'a young homeless spunker', tells O'Casey about her life, which mainly consists in minding her crippled father and drinking methylated spirits (O'Casey, 1945). Millie begins to dance, clearly intoxicated, eventually collapsing in the street. Prior to her collapse, she identifies the British symbolism on a building across the street, 'the massive lion and unicorn frowning down from Hutton's lordly gate ... She sent a venomous spit as high as she could up towards the British arms, twirling round with frantic shakes of her head, letting a yell out of her every few moments' (pp. 86–7). O'Casey concludes she is Cathleen ni Houlihan, an embodiment of the Mother Ireland trope manifesting in the harsh realities of the nascent Irish state of the 1920s; homeless, recently released from a period of incarceration, suffocating from her commitments to a sickly elder generation, seeking psychological escape through substance abuse, easily exploited by those surrounding her and while still beautiful, falling apart for the world to see (pp. 88–9). Millie, who becomes Nannie in O'Casey's play, and returns as Nannie in Lowe's production, was born into chaos, and no structures of society or statehood intervened effectively to alter her life trajectory.

Millie is Nannie, and Lowe has met and lived alongside these women and men growing up in the same part of Dublin and working in prisons and resource centres. These are not people who are born into situations where you can 'go home and eat your dinner with the lights on' (Lowe, 2023). These women have limited choices to find ways to survive and those choices come with risks and consequences, and inevitably, a desire for escape. Her staging of these characters is not to criticise their choices but to question why the same communities remain suffering from the same vulnerabilities a century later. Lowe managed to change her own fortunes, despite experiencing various challenges, but what of her peers from school, neighbours, and wider community circle? What of those fourteen young women from her final school year of eighteen who are no longer alive?

In *The Lost O'Casey*, Lowe physically brings the audiences into this world, where the walls of a theatre building cannot shut out the tougher parts of inner-city life that have become commonplace to ignore. Beginning at the Gate Theatre, this co-production with the Abbey Theatre, co-sponsored by Irish trade unions SIPTU, ICTU and FÓRSA, guided its audience to Dorset St and St Mary's Place, where audiences entered the homes of Lowe's childhood. These homes were not technically her own, with her childhood home already staged in *Basin* (2009) but the homes of her friends and neighbours who provided her with shelter and care during times of difficulty. Through this movement, Lowe and Boss ensured audiences not only felt the ground of the city centre under their feet, but saw the community, the buildings, the sounds, and smells (Lowe and Boss, 2023). ANU's Nannie demonstrated a social system in collapse. It was not the absence of health or cleanliness in any one encounter or space that proved upsetting, but the absence of sufficient care from cradle to grave for an entire community. Likewise, the lack of social workers, police, housing, education, and a sense of functioning governance and social responsibility potentially stimulated a sense of deep unease for the audience member (Lowe and Haughton, 2025). This study situates Nannie as a point of intersection among Lowe's production history and political resonance, resulting in the construction of the Irish state de-homing Ireland's Nannies. As O'Casey articulated to Holloway in 1924, 'there are too many Nannies in the city – they are tragic figures not to be laughed at' (Ayling), his words ghost Lowe's motivations a century later, sometimes consciously, arguably not all the time. These words propel her to rehome Nannies of various periods, illuminating their historical experiences of abandonment, hurt, and injustice by placing these encounters into the public record of conscience. Staging the past in the present is Lowe's strongest suit, and, in so doing, reveals the past as another form of performative construction, legacy, and fluid matrix of power relations and knowledge production.

2.4 Lowe, ANU, and Ghosting the Irish National Narrative

The aesthetics Lowe and Boss create for ANU productions are led by intimacy between audience and historical texture. The set design is the inner city in its ongoing daily routines, and the scenes and encounters they stage in public space traverse between NOW-THEN-NOW in keeping with ANU's leading dramaturgical strategy. In Dublin's inner city, James Little refers to these design choices as an 'aesthetics of dereliction', a type of dramaturgy that gathered momentum following the 2008 economic crash in Ireland, where 'the politics of representation in Irish theatre [. . .] remains "haunted" by the ghost of Sean O'Casey's realist aesthetic' (Little, p. 344). It is not only Lowe and ANU who seem struck by the contemporary energy of O'Casey as Little identifies, also analysing Company SJ's *Fizzle* (2014). Both *Fizzle* and ANU's *Dublin Tenement Experience: Living the Lockout* (2013) used the former tenement building at 14 Henrietta St as a site of performance. For ANU, *Living the Lockout* (Figure 5) returned audiences to the 1913 Dublin Lockout, 'a major industrial dispute between approximately 20,000 workers and 300 employers which took place in Ireland's capital city of Dublin. The dispute lasted from 26 August 1913 to 18 January 1914, and is often viewed as the most severe and significant industrial dispute in Irish history. Central to the dispute was the workers' right to unionise' (*Living the Lockout*, ANU).

In Little's 'scenographic exorcism' (p. 345) he strives to unpack why O'Casey still haunts Irish theatre, providing a close reading of these two contemporary site-responsive performances. Little is right to maintain that 'For those with a background in Irish theatre, the dilapidated frames of once grand Georgian houses immediately call to mind the urban realism that dominates O'Casey's Dublin Trilogy of plays' (p. 347). Sarah Jane Scaife, artistic director of Company SJ, recalls that on entering the 14 Henrietta St building, she instinctively knew demarcating the dramatic space between Beckett's writing in *Fizzles* from the ghost of O'Casey's dramas would be a challenge (p. 346). 14 Henrietta St is a building which 'may contain its own colonial ghosts' (p. 346) built by property developer and MP Luke Gardiner as an eighteenth-century townhouse, with later functions as a legal office, a hostel for the British military in the nineteenth century and rented to families as a tenement dwelling from 1877 to 1979 (p. 346). 'But it was the dramaturgical ghost of O'Casey, that confronted Scaife's company on arrival' (p. 346), Little outlines.

For Lowe, *Living the Lockout* at 14 Henrietta St offered a point of connection between the political stakes of the 1913 Dublin Lockout with the personal

Figure 5 *Living the Lockout* (2013). Performer Lloyd Cooney, Image by Pat Redmond.

impact on individuals and families. In keeping with the overarching perform-ance frame of 'NOW-THEN-NOW', *Living the Lockout* also emphasised how the implications of that historical event linger, haunt, and continue to be affective in the present moment. In another of ANU's 'quirks', performer Laura Murray could trace her grandmother to living in one of the rooms in that tenement building they staged the performance in. Using Murray's grand-mother's letters as source material for the performance, ANU details that documentary material such as this 'are expressive and evocative rather than just explanatory and embody the context, authenticity and dynamics of the Lockout' (ANU). While deeply attuned to the historical record, Lowe's drama-turgy by no means offers an acceptance of the established national historical narrative as an objective, factual, undisputed retelling of events. The Monto Cycle was intended to explore four regeneration attempts in one square mile over a 100-year period, but was not designed for any official state commemor-ation programme. On conclusion of the cycle with *Vardo* in 2014, however, Lowe and ANU's reputation for affective explorations of the recent past through performance was critically acclaimed. As a result, many commissions followed directly connected to Ireland's 'Decade of Centenaries 1912-2023' (DoC).

Lowe and ANU's critical performance work became a leading example of how the narrative construction of the past is reliant on fluctuating dynamics of memory, power networks, and ongoing legacy impact. In Donna Haraway's influential essay 'Situated Knowledges' she critiques the methods and circulation of knowledge production in western systems, particularly the potential for feminism in the 'high stakes tables of the game of contesting public truths' (1988, p. 578). If early public commentary in Ireland underestimated the political potential of commemorative activity during the Decade of Centenaries (Murphy, 2023), arguably conflating commemoration with celebration at times, no such limited interpretations were reported on its conclusion. To query the past is to query the metaphysics that trouble time itself. Indeed, theatre troubles temporality. By staging time in time, so to speak, Lowe's commemorative theatre practice delights in temporal discontinuities and complexities, particularly regarding foundational narratives of modern Irish nationhood. Her body of work at this time staged images, narratives, and affects of the past in the present, and often, enabled these temporal moments to overlap, collide, and collapse. This temporal heterogeneity reminds audiences that time presented as linear experience is indeed constructed and that the theatre's embodied experience is both material and phenomenological. Thus, calendrical and historical appropriations of time, while helpful and significant in terms of building and managing systems of knowledge and modes of interaction, remain contingent on prevailing value-systems. By staging the past in the present and as part of the present, Lowe's work also reminds audiences that what is being commemorated is certainly of significance, yet only potentially of historical accuracy. This archaeology of the past may be the result of personal hauntings that will not subside. It may be the result of contemporary pressures to validate a legacy that continues to prescribe the politics of the day. Regardless, Lowe's commemorative productions trouble temporality and, by staging that tension, confirms that the past is always performative and always in flux.

Another major Lowe production from this DoC period that must be considered here is *Faultline* (2019), developed as part of the Live Collision International Festival 2018 and premiered as part of the Dublin Theatre Festival 2019 while ANU were artists in residence at Dublin's Gate Theatre. *Faultline* (Figure 6) unravelled singular hegemonic nationalist, masculinist and heterosexual constructions of Irish nationhood at a poignant moment of nexus between Ireland's past and present, again, charting a haunted dramaturgy of Ireland's fundamental narratives of nationhood, citizenship, democracy and equality.

Occurring four years following the successful passing of Ireland's Marriage Referendum in 2015, Lowe and ANU's creative producer Lynnette Moran, also

Figure 6 *Faultline* (2019). Performers Matthew Malone and Domhnall
Herdman (holding the phone), Image by Pat Redmond.

co-creator of *Faultline* and founder/director of Live Collision, discuss the
impact of the political campaign in sanitising queer experience in the interests
of convincing the electorate to vote 'yes'. In their interview with Brian Singleton
for *Contemporary Theatre Review*, they discuss the most dangerous year for the
queer community in Ireland: 1982. Singleton outlines:

> On 20 January 1982, RTÉ set designer Charles Self was murdered in his own
> home following a night out in a number of Dublin's main gay venues. To
> this day, no one has been charged. On 8 September 1982, five teenagers attacked
> Declan Flynn in north Dublin and left him for dead. While the men admitted to
> a six-week queer bashing spree in Fairview Park, they all walked free from court,
> having been given suspended sentences for manslaughter. (2021a, pp. 204–5)

Taking this history of violence, secrecy, and exclusion from the official public
sphere as its conceptual space of development in the creative process, Lowe and
Moran consider their role in 'holding the archive' (Singleton, p. 204), which
does not mean accepting all documents and memories as necessarily factual and
comprehensive, but as part of a collage of experiences, sensations, and encounters. In working with a primarily queer creative team who could draw from their
own experiences in varying degrees, Lowe reflects that:

> The thing that struck me the most about if afterwards was in relation to their
> personal archives, to the lads themselves [. . .] in making the choreography,
> we started by using their own personal archive. Each of the moves inside the

score of what they created is built on their personal experiences. So these tiny moments and gestures that I know hold huge stories in terms of their journey to understanding themselves and their sexuality, and their own queer archive is held, is embodied in those ideas and then shared with the rest of them. (p. 209)

Consultation with different generations of queer communities in Ireland was pivotal to constructing the performance, leading to moments of potent connection. In one performance, performer and a founding member of the ANU ensemble, Robbie O'Connor, recollects that in his one-on-one scene with audience members where he is reflecting on being interrogated in a police cell, one audience member interrupted his dialogue to ask, 'Do you see me? Will you hold me?' (p. 210). O'Connor replied that he did see her and then she broke down in tears, and 'that became the moment they spent together and it replaced the scene' (p. 210). LGBTQ+ activist, academic, and author Katherine O'Donnell was involved in the advocacy for gay rights in the 1970s–1980s in Ireland. In discussing her history with the creative team, performer Matthew Malone thanked O'Donnell for her years of campaigning. She asked him his age, and he told he was born in 1993, the year homosexuality was decriminalised in Ireland. O'Donnell's poignant reply, 'We dreamt of you' (p. 207), connects the impact of Lowe's work with ANU to Kavanagh's earlier question, 'How do you catch a dream?' Perhaps the dream can be caught. If memories, language, images, and bodies are enabled to collide, connect, and contradict each other in a space of conceptual, creative, and emotional openness, allowing scenes to be restructured and/or replaced by audience interventions and thus rendering visible '*all* remembering, [and] *not* remembering' (Lowe qtd in Singleton 2021a, p. 206), perhaps wisps of the dream can land in performance. Perhaps the troubled spectre of Irish nationhood can be laid to rest.

Yet how might one catch a dream when performance is swiftly altered from live encounters in public spaces to streamed encounters in digital spaces, as with the onset of COVID-19? Tamara Radak considers how Lowe adapted her craft during the global pandemic in her study of *The Party to End All Parties* (2020), which also situates haunting and the spectral as central to Lowe's work. Drawing from the work of performance scholar Josephine Machon, whose research analyses immersive theatre and site-specific performance, theorising 'live(d) praesent experience' (Mahon, p. 46), Radak considers how this may operate in the context of online performances as a result of COVID-19 lockdowns. In relation to Lowe's work, Radak examines how *The Party to End All Parties* responds to 'the "host/ghost" relationship as a central aspect of site-specific theatre to the virtual realm' (Radak, p. 39) also considering how it activated 'temporal "ghosting"', which blurs the lines between the contemporary setting of lockdown Dublin and this historical landmark of O'Connell bridge as a site inextricably connected to the emergence of Ireland as a republic' (p. 39). Prior to the pandemic, ANU designed its productions for audiences of minimum 1 and maximum approximately 6–8, depending on the specific spatial parameters afforded by each unique site. Overnight, their live-streamed production as part of the Dublin Theatre Festival in 2020 had audiences of thousands. As Lowe reflects in an interview at the time of performance, this production occurring amidst multiple lockdowns invites artists and audiences an opportunity to 'consider ourselves again in terms of [. . .] our connection to the city, to ourselves, to the here and now' (qtd in Radak, p. 41).

Since *The Monto Cycle* premiered in 2010 and including the four productions it consists of, Lowe has directed twenty-two ANU productions during the Decade of Centenaries that respond to the lesser-known histories and individuals of the island. Some of these are specifically commissioned by the Decade of Centenaries, while others were in development entirely separate from state cultural programmes and agendas. Regardless of commissioning processes and contexts, all productions constitute new work directed by Lowe and often written by Lowe. Section 3 of this study offers a close reading of two productions written and directed by Lowe drawing from my time shadowing Lowe in rehearsal for *The Wakefires* (Cork Midsummer Festival, 2022) and *Hammam* (Abbey Theatre 2023–4). Taken as a body of work, what do these productions and processes tell us about Lowe as a theatre artist? What does her body of work reveal about the world we live in, how histories are written and reified, and the potential for theatre to register, reflect and critique power relations today? Haraway's seminal critique pithily provides a response to these questions, demonstrating how political relations can underpin and destabilise knowledge, power, and communities:

> We don't want a theory of innocent powers to represent the world, where language and bodies both fall into the bliss of organic symbiosis . . . but we do need an earthwide network of connections, including the ability partially to translate knowledges among very different – and power-differentiated – communities. We need the power of modern critical theories of how meanings and bodies get made, not in order to deny meanings and bodies, but in order to build meanings and bodies that have a chance for life. (1988, pp. 579–580)

For Lowe's audiences, it is difficult to walk away on conclusion of the performance, assuming one can identify what the point of conclusion is. As the performance encounters are so tightly interwoven in the everyday comings and goings of the site of performance, it is typical for her audiences to linger in those final spaces, waiting to see if another scene will make itself known in the coming moments. During this time, Haraway's insights provoke the questions that I argue Lowe always intends her audiences to consider, 'Vision is *always* a question of the power to see – and perhaps of the violence implicit in our visualizing practices. With whose blood were my eyes crafted?' (p. 585).

3 Unfolding Women's Bodies from Ireland's Violent Past

3.1 Lowe: A Quiet Optimist?

'I have so much information in my body right now, I don't know where to start', Lowe comments on the first day of rehearsals, 9 May 2022, for ANU's *The Wakefires* programmed in the Cork Midsummer Festival 15–26 June 2022 in partnership with the National Museum of Ireland (NMI). Her immediate centralising of her own body as both vestibule and vehicle for knowledge possession and transmission speaks to her dramaturgy for working with others, and, working with the past in the present. From my experience shadowing Lowe in both *The Wakefires* (2022) and *Hammam* (2023–2024), productions that she wrote and directed, it became evident that she begins and ends with the body in terms of how to craft a performance. Firstly, she identifies which bodies from history they will 'summon' for performance (Lowe, Haughton rehearsal notes 2022). Through this return to those bodies from the past, Lowe asks her audiences to reconsider the history that they know and have been taught. In this moment of Irish centenary commemorations (2012–2023) which revisits how the founding of the modern Irish state is inextricably linked with war, her work poses significant questions that one may wish to avoid, such as, was it right, was it worth it, and how might it still be prescribing experience, identity and politics today?

This section presents analysis of *The Wakefires* and *Hammam,* productions which centre on the Irish Civil War (1922–1923) that broke out following the narrow ratification of the Anglo-Irish Treaty in the Dáil [government] on 7 January 1922 which ultimately split the Republican movement. The Treaty proposed 'the withdrawal of British troops from the majority of the country, but gave dominion status to Ireland rather than that of an independent Republic, retained the Oath of Allegiance to the British Crown, and provided for the establishment of a Boundary Commission to create a border between the Irish Free State and the Northern counties which opted to remain under British rule' (NMI). Irish studies scholar Síobhra Aiken outlines the tensions inherent in processes of remembering the various stages of Irish revolution against British rule versus remembering the Irish Civil War, drawing from political debate stemming back to ancient Greece:

> If revolution offered enlightenment and reinvigoration, then civil war was an embarrassing reminder of the possible regression of mankind. Indeed, this binary between honourable revolution and best-forgotten civil war is perhaps the defining feature of the commemorative narrative of the Irish revolution and its aftermath (Aiken, 2022b).

Stepping into this murky territory of the 'best-forgotten civil war' as Aiken coins it, this analysis returns to Schneider's concept of 'unfolding of the body' (1997, p. 2) through art as this approach underscores how Lowe works with performers, place, and history in to tell these conflicted histories, records, and memories.

Though surrounded by historical debate and analysis through regular media commentary, in rehearsals, Lowe does not look for 'a beginning', demonstrating no such innocence regarding neatly written linear histories championing victors vs losers, perpetrators vs victims, in convenient beginning-middle-end structures. Rather, she is drawn to the point of connection among various points of departure regarding a historical event or encounter, revelling in the theatrical possibilities for staging those contested truths, contradictions, inconclusive accounts, cultural mapping, human failures and frailties that emerge from the records and at times, lack of records, depending on the events in question. Most of all, Lowe is as generous in her staging of the everyday acts of love, hope and connection as she is to those infamous moments of historical tragedy. This realisation surprised me while in the rehearsal room for both *The Wakefires* and *Hammam*. Despite more than a decade experiencing her productions, my default critical position tended to theorise ANU's works written and directed by Lowe pertaining to traumatic events that the individual or community suffered more so than their capacity for resilience, care and potential recovery, renewal or transcendence.

Gesturing to emotional connection and generosity of the human spirit in performance, against all the odds, reveals a quiet optimism regarding Lowe's own faith in the power of community and co-presence, easily overlooked through her body of work situated among decades of ongoing war. In performance, these moments of care enable audiences to register, or 'confront' as Crowe concluded, the violence and trauma that are inescapable when revisiting modern Irish history, a narrative of nationhood that emerged from violence in intensely localised contexts. Often, one encounter that is dripping in the bloodshed of Ireland's past is immediately followed by another encounter that softly demonstrates intimacy among parents and children, neighbours and friends, or, indeed, revolutionaries and soldiers from oppositional sides. The sense of love, hope,

Figure 7 *The Wakefires* (2022). Performers Úna Kavanagh and Ella Lily Hyland, Image by Pat Redmond.

and connection may be difficult to see at times amidst the energetic performance of historical tragedies and traumas; however, it is there. It emerges very gently, such as with two performers showing each other care by sharing food, offering touch or the cleaning of wounds. It may also be sought from the audience through performers asking them for assistance or a question, challenging the audience member to decide whether to offer comfort, ignorance, or complicity. The significance of care, co-presence, and community is centralised in this forthcoming subsection examining *The Wakefires* (Figure 7), a production which tells the stories of violence against women often colluded in by women, though in the context of conflicts initiated by men.

3.2 *The Wakefires*: A Fevered Dream

In its opening premise, a scene between Mary Carey, played by Úna Kavanagh, and her daughter Máire/Maura Carey, played by Ella Hyland, introduces the audience to the Irish Civil War and its impact on families and communities primarily, rather than governments or armies. The site of per-formance is Elizabeth Fort, originally constructed in 1601 and used as a British Army barracks until the early twentieth century, before operating as a Garda station following Irish independence (Elizabeth Fort History, Cork City). On arrival, the audience meet Mary running to one of the small houses on the barracks site with her daughter's coat. She desperately pounds the door trying to find out if her daughter is inside so she can give her the coat, asking the audience to assist her. An Irish Free State soldier, Seán McGrath, played by Matthew Williamson, refuses to confirm if her daughter is there and urges her to go home. He responds harshly to her, his voice pregnant with violent potential, but eventually concedes to take the coat and give it to her daughter. Perhaps he recognises that this matrilineal line of connection between mother and daughter may possess greater force than the newly minted authority afforded him by the patriarchal structures of military. Mary reveals the recent events that brought them here:

> She' oney wearin' her underwear . . . they dragged her, you see, from her bed. Last night. Midnight. [. . .] They . . . they've been roundin' up cumann na mBan women all across the city, so's no surprise they come for her. Sure they've been tormentin' her since they got here, day in day out, never givin' her a minutes peace for the last 8 months. First place they come on the first day, our shop. The fuckers landed on us 'cause they knew exactly where to go,- sure we'd been hidin' enough of them in the tan war for them to know where to go, an They've turned worse even than the savages that went before them. (*The Wakefires* Show Document, pp. 3–4)

Lowe's opening dialogue achieves a multitude: the audience are informed of the historical moment of the Irish Civil War in which pro-Treaty forces fought anti-Treaty forces less than six months following the conclusion of the War of Independence (1919–1921) when Irish republican soldiers fought the British Army in challenge of British rule in Ireland. The audience are also told that the manner in which women as well as men were caught and imprisoned was violent, but most significantly, the point is made that this performance and history is about families torn apart throughout the island of Ireland, exemplified by Mary's plea to know the fate of her daughter. Fundamentally, this performance instils the message that the audience matters (Lowe, 2013), just as social responsibility matters, ideas which may seem obvious but are easily forgotten in contemporary neoliberal cultures that craft competition as the driving force underpinning social interaction, value, and worth. Perhaps this audience can help her locate her daughter, but perhaps not. That will be revealed through the decision of each audience member in how they respond, reminding them that while the situation is not within their control, their response to the situation is. How one chooses to respond to situations of human suffering is arguably one of the most significant decisions any individual can make within their lifetime, and Lowe's body of work excels in underscoring that through the 'ethical encounters' (Lowe, 2012) she stages.

Later, the same soldier features in a scene set prior to the outbreak of the Civil War, as Lowe curates her scenes to be read like a 'poem written backwards' as

Kavanagh identifies (Kavanagh, 2024). This time, his wounds are being tended to by the same mother and daughter the audience met on arrival, but the dramatised temporal moment has been rewound to his involvement in the War of Independence against the British forces, in particular, the 'black and tan' army, notorious for 'brutality' and 'reprisals against civilians' (Lowe, 2004). They are inside the Carey's shop located on Washington St in Cork, a street familiar with intense violence in the War of Independence during 'the burning of Cork' (11–12 December 1920, O'Keeffe). Seeds of romance between the Irish soldier McGrath and the young Máire are insinuated through coy looks and flirtatious smiles, knowingly observed by her mother Mary. However, as quickly as that moment of budding connection emerges, it is then snatched away: noise breaks out, new performers burst into the space, and a devastating movement sequence suggests the repeated assault of Máire. Audience members are hurriedly pushed into other spaces and/or separated, and the narrative returns to violence once more in a performance style Lowe visualises as a 'fevered dream' (Haughton rehearsal notes, 2022).

Lowe is not staging a documentary play, but staging sensations of the past derived from the fractured records that remain. The loss of intimacy in this way offers a double blow; not only has violence erupted but the hope emanating from that moment of human connection, or communion, has been lost. Those who have lived through political violence and, indeed, domestic violence, understand this performance structure. There may be breaks from the tension and the torture, but they are temporary. While power is abused, peace is only ever momentary. *The Wakefires* and indeed *Hammam* show their audiences how co-existence with violence is exhausting, constantly waiting for it to end, and, to begin again. Within those modest moments of respite however, Lowe shows the potential for renewal, and thus, a quiet optimism among her own value systems.

The origin point for *The Wakesfires* is as visceral as its eventual performance. 'Has Brenda [Malone] shown you what she has in the freezer?' Crowe asks Lowe in 2018. Malone, Curator of Military History at the National Museum of Ireland (NMI), brings Lowe to the NMI to show her women's hair forcibly removed during an 'Outrage' in the Irish Civil War (Figure 8). 'Outrage'[d] women occupy a space in Ireland's past, but not always in Ireland's history books, an absence being challenging by scholars and communities alike. Historian Mary McAuliffe summarises how Outrages spanned from 'a multitude of incidents during this period, varying on arms raids on homes and burnings (of dwellings, outhouses, or crops) to the stealing of livestock and other possessions, in addition to sexual assaults and other attacks on women' (2023, p. 82). Lowe is sensitive to these women's discomfort in stating explicitly the nature of violence inflicted on them, which lends to her method of embodied encounters framing the performance style

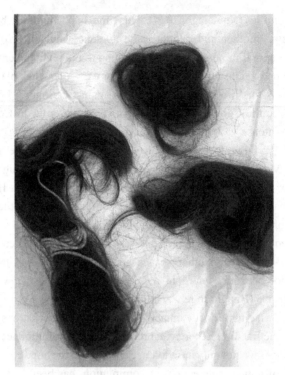

Figure 8 Female Hair forcibly removed during an 'Outrage' in the Irish Civil War, courtesy of the National Museum of Ireland Ireland and the Kevin Barry Family.

rather than extensive narrative exposition. Lowe recalls, 'It's also sad to read of the attempts the women made to protect themselves, even later in giving statements. They had no words for what happened to them physically; the language could be very reticent' (qtd in *Irish Times*, 2022). This point is further examined by McAuliffe, noting, ' … anti treaty women were often arrested and held for days in local barracks where they suffered what they referred to as indignities. This obtuse language covers what were sometimes serious physical and sexual assaults. The later military pension application files of many these women indicate that their mental, physical and/or emotional health was seriously, sometimes permanently damaged by these experiences' (*The Wakefires* Programme Note, 2022).

The shaved hair that Malone displayed for Lowe and the act of brutality it symbolised commits her creative intentions to rehoming these ghosts, similar to her sense of loyalty to staging Ireland's Nannies as explored in Section 2. It brought her to scrutinise military archives which revealed that many of the women prominent in Ireland's revolutionary period may have suffered an Outrage for loyalty to a chosen side, and later, refused a pension from the

Irish Free State, suffering lifelong economic disadvantage in addition to the wounds accumulated through war (Coleman, 2017). In this production, Lowe stages 'sister against sister' in a historical event predominantly characterised as 'brother against brother' (Connolly, 2021, p. 151) through a series of performative episodes that are challenging to observe. The site of Elizabeth Fort is staged as the period in between capture and transportation of these anti-Treaty women to Dublin's Kilmainham and Mountjoy Jails, and incarceration at the North Dublin Union (NDU). The women captured are alleged members of Cumann na mBan, the Irish women's anti-Treaty organisation working in support of the Irish Republican Army (IRA) as they did during the War of Independence. Their political stance is in opposition to Cumann na Saoirse, the Irish women's pro-Treaty organisation who support the recently formed Irish Government, many of whom also fought in the War of Independence. The provocation lingers for the audience: if the bedrock of national independence for twenty-six out of thirty-two counties is built upon a division of communities, betrayal of kin, bodily violation, and destruction of property, then what kind of nation can develop? The bitter, fractured nature of the fighting cannot be overestimated, nor its intergenerational impact on social, political, and familial relationships.

In this production, as with much of her previous work, Lowe draws from oral histories of persons not well known or established in canonical history, but whose existence, actions, and subsequent omissions directly informed the historical trajectory of the island of Ireland. Presenting this to audiences is not intended as nostalgic provocation but an opportunity to engage in renewed analysis of assumed knowledge typically embedded in educational and political rhetoric. 'The Famine was only nine Mammies ago' Lowe muses during a discussion in rehearsals regarding intergenerational trauma and epigenetics (Haughton rehearsal notes, 2022). How might impulses and behaviour(s) be shaped by the scars of that national tragedy when an island of eight million became an island of six million between 1845 and 1852? (Ó Murchadha, 2011). Indeed, tracing this history through the matrilineal line demonstrates her own instincts to discover women's history, not always easily accessible in a country that privileges male narratives, names, and desires. These references to tragedies and gender politics are the larger critical context that frames the rehearsal process from which the choreography of intimate encounters with the audience is developed. If history is about victors, then Lowe's work is certainly not history. However, it is about the past, and she reveals a certain compulsion to unearth it, revisit it, acknowledge what has been suppressed or silenced, and, ultimately, restory it.

The Wakefires operated through staging action in two houses in Elizabeth Fort. Beginning at the entry to the Fort, the first audience group of four people (maximum) are led to House 1 known as 'The Summonings' where the action is set on 28 February 1923, before moving to House 2 'The Happenings' set on 23 June 1923. The mother–daughter relationship of Mary–Máire Carey is pivotal to both houses, detailing the grim undoing of their family unit due to shifting allegiances from a collective Irish republican army challenging British rule to a split republican movement during the Irish civil war, referred to as 'anti-Treaty' and 'pro-Treaty'. The performance follows through this macro-narrative of split national allegiances to a micro-narrative exploring the story of oppositional female revolutionary organisations Cumann na mBan and Cumann na Saoirse. Nan Fennell, played by Kate Finnegan, is a Cumann na Saoirse member held captive with Cumann na mBan members, Máire Carey (Hyland), Ellen Walsh (Gillian McCarthy) and Birdie [Bridie/Brigit] Fitzgerald (Sarah Morris) in House 1 'The Summonings'. '"Cumann na searchers" comin' here to spy on us' (Show Document, p. 18) is the accusation levelled by Máire [Hyland] as Nan's [Finnegan] allegiance is suspected, while Birdie [Morris] paints a picture of women's experiences at this time. Birdie signals the hardship they faced from former peers and comrades in which they suffered various forms of violence, as well as their active military role motivated by fervent political beliefs, in which they willingly and consciously conspired in acts of violence directed at others.

Lowe does not enable easy audience sympathy for any singular person or party in her scenes, displaying instead a sense of endless retaliation and suspicion among families and communities, with no clear resolution in sight. Birdie tells the audience 'People who know me call me Birdy, as in a little birdy told me . . . cause, like I'm always havin' to pass on . . . (information)' (p. 10.) In the next breath she lightens the atmosphere in the dark, cramped performance space, adding 'Though, I prefer to think of a birdy as a kiss, y'know, like, give us a birdy, now I'm not asking you for a birdy, don't worry, but I am a good kisser' (p. 10). She concludes her introduction of her story to the audience by pointing to how she became active in the revolutionary movement, detailing, 'It was Sr. Brigid above in the convent who made a revolutionary out of me. Sr. Brigid made revolutionaries out of the lot of us to be fair' (p. 11). Through this brief commentary, Lowe takes her audience from the intimate relationship between split communities back to the wider social context of the war, in which many communities and organisations became implicated in one way or another, including those whose primary purpose is to spread teachings of peace and harmony.

The Wakefires centres on specific women involved in the Irish Civil War 1922–1923, and the consequences of their participation. This history is often spoken of in hushed voices among Irish communities, yet Aiken's *Spiritual*

Wounds (2022a) challenges a blanket generalisation of silence regarding the war crimes from this period. There is little common ground among Irish and British forces at this point in history, yet the shared experience that does emerge is how both sides relied upon the violation of women as a tactic of war, and, thus, ANU is explicit in highlighting this violence as one of the centre points from which the Irish Free State emerged. As Birdie describes her physical and mental state to the audience, 'I can't sleep but I'm so tired, can't eat but I'm hungry, my stomach is in knots like, cramping, jolting like it's trying to hurt me from the inside out' (p. 22). She prompts the audience to consider the impact on women, stating, 'They talk of the toll on the men ... What about the women? I've never once heard anyone talk about the toll on us ... Have you?' (p. 23). It provokes the question once more: if an entity is born from violence and, indeed, gendered violence, what capacity for peace and equality might it possess? McAuliffe confirms these suggestions of violent encounters for women at that time:

> [...], pro or anti, treaty, women were attacked by all sides, Irregular Republicans or the pro Treaty National Army ... During these months of 1922–23 over 600 anti-treaty women were arrested and imprisoned ... they were stripped, kicked, beaten and assaulted by warders, soldiers and Cumann na Saoirse women ... ' (*The Wakefires* Programme Note, 2022)

The violence against women during this period is becoming more well known through scholarly interventions by Irish feminist historians, sociologists, and artists often framed by the Decade of Centenaries programme (DoC). Despite the sensitivity of the material and the explicit violence it references, *The Wakefires* sold out in a matter of hours (Cork Midsummer Festival, 2022), signalling a public appetite to engage with this history, difficult as it may be.

Lowe keeps the female characters specific to women primarily involved in the Cumann na mBan network throughout Cork and its neighbouring regions, as Cork is the county which experienced the most violence at this time. Birdie [Bridget] Fitzgerald, for example, a key figure from the Cumann na mBan (Aiken, 2022b), presented in *The Wakefires* carried what was described as 'a parcel of bombs', taking guns, ammunition, and messages 'from street to street, village to village, hiding IRA men on the run' (Lowe qtd in *Irish Times*, 2022). Aiken recalls the later suffering Fitzgerald experienced as a result of her participation, developing what she termed 'a weakness' and 'lost the power of her hands and of speech for a short time' (2022). Aiken also notes the gendered responses of the Irish Military Service Pensions Board when reviewing female submissions for a pension based on service provided during the Revolutionary period, noting their policy to send '"nervous" female applicants for gynaeco-logical testing' (2022). Head-shaving and other humiliations, physical and sexual assault, and economic discrimination paint a harrowing picture of Irish women's experience as part of the road to national independence, with their contributions and legacies poorly captured in the modern Irish state. Productions such as *The Wakefires* become potent landmarks in a shift in public discourse by not only paying tribute to these women but also demonstrating the level of intense curation involved in the writing of canonical Irish history in the first place.

Trepidation preceded Ireland's Decade of Centenaries from many quarters and throughout national dialogue as a result of the sensitive histories it would illuminate. Irish sociologist Linda Connolly pithily captures this tension, asking, 'Who will be remembered?' (2021, p. 150). Connolly proposes that historical remembering should be as much informed by ethical imperatives as record-keeping. The Irish state's treatment of women in the twentieth century and attempts at commemoration of women's experience in the twenty-first century are as fragmented and uneven as those burned archives from the 1922 bombing of the Four Courts, archives spanning 1174–1922 (McCann, BBC NI). Embers remain from the blaze, but it is a challenge to visualise them as whole and unscarred. These discriminations are strengthened by structural inequalities found in the operations of state and society. Connolly outlines, 'The gulf that has existed between the established history (that of "heroes") and women's (hidden) history in Irish studies [. . .] still persists. In Irish universities, over eighty per cent of the professoriate in Irish history are men and only thirty women have been elected to the current Dáil [government], out of one hundred and sixty seats' (p. 150). Connolly outlines the stakes involved in this commemorative moment: 'if violence cuts to the very heart of the State's foundation, how and in what ways is this gendered? And why was the violence women experienced marginalised, minimised or negated in the official histories of this period for such a long time?' (p. 152) Connolly's potent questioning of the crafting of Irish history is where *The Wakefires*, written and directed by Lowe, begins its work.

The subject matter is of great personal care to Lowe and everyone in the room, from performers and designers to producers and company/stage managers. Such a statement can easily be made in advance of all productions; however, this is not another production of a canonical play, but original new work that offers both the opportunity for the ensemble to possess greater agency in crafting the work, and thus ownership of it, in addition to the sense of reconnecting with one's own past. Phone calls home by the ensemble to family members were not uncommon during rehearsals, trying to establish which side(s) their ancestors may have taken, and what level of familial participation may have occurred in the battles of the time (Haughton Rehearsal Notes, 2022). If a passer-by were to enter her rehearsal room for this production, they would easily be forgiven for wondering if they had wandered into a history seminar.

ANU's overarching methodology of 'NOW-THEN-NOW' manifests as a sense of 'looped temporalities' (Kelly et al., 2020, p. 7) that reinvigorate historical acts and question their ongoing impact on the present in various forms. The audience and Lowe's ensemble begin from 'now', the present moment. They are immersed into 'then', always constructed creatively from historical document, artefact, and oral testimony, and are finally returned to 'now' at the end of the performance, by which time, it rarely feels like an ending but perhaps a portal into a different kind of 'now', a present that feels markedly different from 60 to 90 minutes previous.

Day 1 of rehearsals poses a stark question: Ireland emerged due to the 'pro-Treaty' side winning. Had the anti-Treaty side prevailed, what kind of society and state would exist? Everyone in the rehearsal room is born in Ireland and of Irish nationality, and conversations explore whether life might be different had the anti-Treaty side won. At the time of rehearsals in May 2022, Irish society was confronting a housing crisis, health crisis, education crisis, economic crisis post-COVID with the latest recession looming, and ongoing political crisis in the north of Ireland as a result of Brexit. At the time of going to press in 2025, many of those crises remain. Suggesting an alternative vision could have resulted in something better is attractive and seductive but can only exist in the discursive realm of 'what if'. If theatre is considered a mirror up to nation, as Martin Esslin and Christopher Murray proclaim (Esslin, 1976; Murray, 1997), then Lowe's practice is a mirror up to the Irish Free State. The Irish Free State signed the Anglo-Irish Treaty which accepted that six counties in the north of Ireland would remain within British direct rule, anticipating it as a 'stepping stone' (Dáil Éireann Debate, 7 January 1922) to lead to full independence eventually. Since that time, the space between the 26-county state and the 6-county northern Irish state achieving unification peacefully has become more and more distant. *The Wakefires* thus confronts how the Irish Free State became constituted as an inherently disrupted entity awaiting a more harmonious future that might not materialise.

Like much of Lowe's practice, *The Wakefires* is a work fuelled by curiosity and discontent in equal measure. Lowe's potent ability to capture the type of violence perpetuated against women in Ireland resonates as cuttingly in this production as it did in *Laundry*: emotional, physical and sexual wounds suppressed for generations, revealing a lineage of stigma and trauma within the communities and families subjected to it. Once more, women's bodies are rendered sacrificial in the name of patriarchal nationhood further embroiled in conservative Roman Catholic ideologies. Early twentieth-century Irish theatre expressed similar political instincts to Lowe, as already examined in Section 2 relating to the plays and motivations of Seán O'Casey. At this time, the formation of the Irish Literary Theatre (established in 1899), among other nationalist artistic and cultural pursuits, took place, directly intertwined with the colonial and revolutionary politics dominating the time. Observing Lowe at work 100 years on, that spirit of revolution seems very much alive. It is not a reckoning with the British Empire however, but one with the current problematic 26-county state and 36-county island, exploited and vulnerable, still carrying the burden of unresolved histories inextricably linked with the foundation of the state.

Sarah Morris, playing Bridie Fitzgerald, stumbles across the phrase in her research on the split in the women's revolutionary movement, 'Inadequate in your loyalty for Ireland' (Morris qtd in Haughton rehearsal notes, 2022). This statement is a key point of creative departure for Morris. She leaps on the phrase, seeking to unwield it, understand it, and create from it. I suspect she would crawl inside those words if she could, just to find the most potent method of capturing it for performance. The desire by all the performers to retrieve the remnants of their matrilineal heritage is palpable. There is a sustenance in learning how their foremothers lived and the choices they made. It is like a hunger for food they never tasted before. There is a feeling of loyalty towards women they have never met, regardless of their deeds and wants. Many were victimised but they did not see themselves as victims, and, indeed, caused violence and harm to others. The energy in the room provokes many thoughts at this time of national and nationalist volatility both domestically and globally. Would I be adequate in my loyalty for Ireland I wonder? What does that even mean today? Indeed, is the Irish state 'adequate' in its treatment of all its citizens? Lowe says she gets a sense of how each production will be in advance of it finding its feet. 'The air will be thick for this one' (Lowe, Haughton rehearsal notes, 2022). It was. It remained thick for the next one, *Hammam*, as the dust of recently bombed buildings filled the mouths of the audience stumbling through the 'rubble' of the Peacock, the underground performance venue at the Abbey Theatre, transformed into the site of the Battle of Dublin just over a century ago.

3.3 *Hammam:* 'That's My Souvenir' Sarah Kirwan, Irish Citizen Army, July 1922

Sarah Kirwan, Irish revolutionary, applied for a military pension to the Irish Free State for her claims of military service with the Irish Citizen Army (ICA) between 1916 and 1923, a period which experienced the Easter Rising (1916), the War of Independence (1919–1921), and, finally, the Civil War (1922–23). Her claim for a pension was rejected (Military Service Pensions Collection 1916–1923). Her 'souvenir' for her service is something quite unexpected instead. As the audience follows various performers run, dance, attack, and collide through a transformed Peacock theatre including its dressing rooms, greenroom and technical spaces, ANU's final Decade of Centenaries-led production, co-produced with the Abbey Theatre, charts the concluding battle of Ireland's violent past, 'the Battle of Dublin', through the double lens of the individual and the nation. In Kirwan's words, written by Lowe and performed by Sarah Morris, her souvenir is 'An' imbecile child/An' a sick husband/An' a knock on the head [. . .] That's my souvenir from those tan times' (*Hammam* show document, p. 16). The child she speaks of here is not from her husband, but a pro-Treaty soldier 'Isaiah' (played by Peter Rothwell) just captured by the anti-Treaty battalion she is working with as a nurse in the makeshift field hospital in the hotel.

The Hammam Hotel was part of the block of hotels utilised by the anti-Treaty IRA near Dublin's main thoroughfare O'Connell St (Gillis, 2023), while the anti-Treaty IRA executive had taken over The Four Courts which housed the Public Record Office of Ireland comprising seven centuries of Ireland's history (Gittins, 2022). The Four Courts were a symbol of the Republic, and its occupation on 1 July 2022 is considered the starting point for the Irish Civil War (Gillis, 2011, 2023). Some of the IRA occupying the Four Courts at this time also occupied it during the 1916 Easter Rising against British rule in Ireland, and were now fighting against their former comrades in arms. During this Battle of Dublin, the anti-Treaty force occupying the Four Courts blew it up, and, along with it, the written records of Ireland's ancient and recent past (Gillis, 2023). The block of hotels were considered a strategic misstep by the anti-Treaty movement, as it allowed the National Army to encircle them and close in. The National Army consisted of pro-Treaty soldiers and their defence of the city was bolstered by the weapons provided by the British army (Gillis, 2011), the same colonial force they had spent the previous decade and, indeed, centuries, fighting against.

Returning to Kirwan (Morris), through her interactions with Isaiah (Rothwell), Lowe underscores the intensely localised nature of the Civil War, instilling a century of political friction and divisive cultural memory thereafter. In this encounter, it is revealed that during the recently concluded War of Independence, Isaiah had stayed in Kirwan's family home operating as a safe house where she tended to his wounds. She reminds him he was there for ' . . . two nights. Caught between two walls, I said soft things to ye' (*Hammam* show document, p. 15). As Isaiah's eyes meet Kirwan's, the space between them appears to shrink as Kirwan removes her cardigan to reveal a blouse with damp patches from her lactating breasts. The wetness of her blouse captures the tragedy of the various wars in a simple, yet evocative, gesture. If she is breastfeeding a child conceived with him, then what is the distance between their past intimacy and present opposition? Will that child nurse from their mother again? The duration of a pregnancy is all the time it took for a nation to become splintered. Women's bodies once more tell a history not often captured in historical accounts nor compensated by institutional authorities. Lovers are now enemies, and many children are orphaned or abandoned depending on whether a family exists who can mind them. Though we learn that she has other young children and a sick husband dependent on her, Kirwan refuses to leave the Hammam Hotel along with her female comrades despite orders to do so from their male superiors, declaring, 'We get to say when we say when' (p. 18). Assured of military failure in this endeavour, all these women have left is their power to refuse, and that shall not be taken from them in Lowe's production, as she keeps faith with their clearly stated principles regardless of their inevitable doom from former comrades across the battle lines.

As in *The Wakefires*, Lowe ensures the consequences for those principles are clearly communicated in performance. Kirwan (Morris), Flinter (played by Ghaliah Conroy), and Kathy Barry (played by Ella Hyland), discuss what can happen to revolutionary women caught by the opposing side:

ANNIE	(if) They have their way | We'all be like Mary Murphy?
SARAH	Yeh.
KATHY	Who?
ANNIE	in (19)13 in Jacobs
SARAH	Sent her to a laundry.
KATHY	A laundry laundry?
SARAH	*(ironically)* no
ANNIE	Soon as we stick our head up above the parapet – there's no one speakin' for us – no borstals for girls like us. |
SARAH	Arrested on the strike line she was
ANNIE	– they sent her to a Magdalene laundry.

(*Hammam* show document pp. 18–19)

In this brief exchange, Lowe returns her audience to the infrastructure of the Irish Free State that existed following the surrender of the anti-Treaty forces. While laundries and institutions existed prior to the establishment of the Irish Free State, their quantity and significance grew exponentially in its wake. Twentieth-century Ireland possessed the largest institutionalised population in the world, where vulnerable women, men, and children were sent to institutions in harsh conditions for varying lengths of time (Smith, 2007; O'Sullivan and O'Donnell, 2012). Through this dialogue Lowe also returns her audiences to *The Monto Cycle* which features *World End's Lane* (2010) and *Laundry* (2011), interconnected productions that reveal the collision of political, social, and religious forces offering nuanced encounters of everyday life for women, children and vulnerable communities in Dublin's north inner city.

Hammam is conceived from 'the epicentre of the Civil War and a nation teetering on the brink of peace' (ANU/*Hammam*). Records detail that 'The billiard room in the Hammam Hotel was designated as the garrison's hospital and the hotels were well stocked with food. The garrison comprised 70 men and 30 women' (Ó Corráin and Hanley, RTÉ). The attacks on the hotel were severe:

> The Hammam Hotel was shelled by an 18-pounder gun from the corner of Henry Street and the force of the explosions smashed many windows in the surrounding area. Once the shells cut through the hotel walls, armoured cars pulled up outside and poured fire through the breach with Lewis machine-guns. This pattern of shelling followed by close-quarter machine-gun fire was repeated. Some twenty-five shells were fired at the republican garrison, causing enormous damage. Despite the obvious danger, hundreds of onlookers watched the final hours of the siege, and several were injured by sniper fire. The attack continued until midnight (Ó Corráin and Hanley, RTÉ).

With a clear picture of the devastation outside the hotel captured in detail, Lowe's production imagines the picture inside the hotel, what it looked like, smelled like, and felt like. It was a site of both physical and psychological doom, an endgame to the previous decade of revolutions, where soldiers, medics, and priests were 'Facing former comrades for refusing to surrender to a half baked republic minus its promised equality' (O'Rourke, 2023). Theatre critic Una Mullally reflects on *Hammam*'s 'series of remarkable moments in an often overwhelmingly compelling experience' in her *Irish Times* review, noting:

> Within this maze-like spectacle – Where are we? Which direction are we going in? Is there any way out at all? – Louise Lowe, the production's writer and director, remains fiercely attentive to detail and to the visceral human experience of history. Collapses and circuit-breakers occur constantly: Ghaliah Conroy's breath-holding movement in one striking piece of choreography; Darragh Feehely's strange and beautiful monk; Robbie O'Connor's remarkable embodiment of a stoic rebel suppressing panic; Úna Kavanagh's capacity to imbue the strange with calm. (Mullally, 2023)

Honing in on intimacy and visceral connection in performance, eight audiences members enter the space split into two groups of four that are led by different performers moving around the site, including the entrance and hallways, the Turkish bath at the centre point of the Hammam Hotel, the hotel bar, a hotel bedroom, and another room transformed into the makeshift hospital. Irish revolutionary Marie Perolz (played by Úna Kavanagh) works in the hospital with Kirwan and Flinter, and is tending to a wounded anti-Treaty soldier Christy Crowley (played by Matthew Williamson) as the audience enters. The dimly lit

Figure 9 *Hammam* (2023–2024). Performer Ghaliah Conroy, Image by Ros
Kavanagh.

space reeks of disinfectant, dust, and old air. The modest surfaces in the space
are covered with first-aid materials and war propaganda. Shrapnel from an
explosion is stuck in Crowley's eye, and Perolz is trying to remove it. Flinter
tells the audience, 'His eye. She's after lickin' out the shrapnel an' the glass after
it got exploded' (p. 6). Lowe is quick to exploit the queasiness of the revelation,
with Perolz asking the audience members, 'Can you see any shards?' (p. 7),
knowing that not one single audience member wants to take a closer look at his
mutilated face. Moments later, a grenade is thrown through a window, landing
in the modest space for the audience to sit and stand. The audience are rushed to
the next room, reminded that a century ago, their forebears were standing in
those very conditions, but the grenade was real, as were the casualties.

Some of the cruelties of the Civil War cannot be captured in language or
played via realist aesthetics, and in their place, Lowe stages choreography that
expresses the NOW-THEN-NOW dramaturgy central to framing ANU's productions. Conroy's solo dance piece (Figure 9) begins in the vein of traditional
Irish dancing, building to the stylised movements more associated with the
tradition of a whirling dervish and thus, the potential for transcendence. She is

later accompanied in this movement sequence by Williamson and their bodies align as they bend and stretch, contort and spasm. Their initial choreography evokes the seeds of a beautiful dream and a sacred belief that was national independence, based on peace, community, and equality. That dream was extinguished by decades of war, and in its place, the nightmare of the Civil War is met by the escalation of their pulsating bodies – frantic, chaotic, and in pain. Faith in the master narratives of nationhood, religion, and family has not secured their victory nor provided safety. *Hammam* is as dark in its philosophical provocations as it is with showcasing the physical torture many suffered, prompting the question – what is left to believe in?

Through the grenades, guns, and dread of inevitable surrender staged throughout the performance, Lowe's brief moments of respite and hope glimmer through. Water becomes a potent visual strategy she relies on to signal release from torment. As Kirwan recognises the soldier who impregnated her, she leaps toward him with a gun. Stopped by her comrades, she tries to explain her actions, asking the audience:

SARAH	(To the audience) How far away is it to the seaside?
ANNIE	What?
SARAH	The seaside	
ANNIE	Which seaside?
SARAH		How far away?
ANNIE	Why?
SARAH	I want to go to the sea.
SARAH	I don't know where else to put me pain.

(*Hammam* Show Document, p. 19)

The pain stems from not only the recent days and weeks in the Battle of Dublin, but the years of suffering she has endured while active in the revolutionary movement. Evidently, Kirwan has demonstrated bravery, sacrifice, and loyalty, but there are limits to her resilience. If the expanse of the sea is large enough and deep enough to hold her pain, maybe she can experience healing, learning to live again rather than struggling to survive.

Water also offers solace to established Irish Republican and anti-Treaty leader Cathal Brugha (played by Jamie O'Neill) in the moments prior to his death (Figure 10), considered the first high-profile fatality of the Civil War (Ó Corráin and Hanley, 'an extraordinary life cut short' 2022b). He removes his shoes and socks, placing his bare feet into a bowl of water for a moment's respite and perhaps, a reference to the Catholic ritual of washing feet, as Jesus did for his twelve disciples the night before his death (Jones, 'Holy Week'). According to historical debate, Brugha understands the likely fatal outcome of his decision to exit the Hammam Hotel amidst the fighting. However, his hope

Figure 10 *Hammam* (2023–2024). Performer Darragh Feehely and Úna Kavanagh, Image by Ros Kavanagh. All rights to ANU images are retained by ANU Productions.

was that his death may prevent further deaths, particularly from comrade turned on comrade, though his hope did not manifest (Ó Corráin and Hanley, 'an indomitable spirit' 2022c). Signalling his intention to the audience from his scene's outset, he *'takes off a miraculous medal on a blue string. He hands it to an audience member',* instructing them gently, 'Afterwards, 'em ... in case, ya know? anythin' should (happen)' (*Hammam* Show Document, p. 31). His faith is centre stage in his scenes, revisiting his belief in their political position with the priest Fr Dominic O'Connor (played by Darragh Feehely) prior to his exit. In a quiet and understated moment, Brugha exits the Hotel and the audience (certainly the Irish audience members), know that something did happen, and, did not cause any dent in the fighting and fatalities to come.

Water dominates the scenography in many ways, as the transformed Peacock space of long corridors, rubble, and dark twists and turns, eventually leads the audience to the centre point of the space, the Turkish bath, filled with a shallow sprinkle of water. Evidently, the impact of this bath and its connotations for purification, healing, and potential transformation or transcendence, links the secular to the sacred in Lowe's conceptualisation of this performance. In this space of shallow water, Fr Dominic O'Connor stands naked and alone, proclaiming his readiness for the end. Fr O'Connor was born John O'Connor in 1883 to a devout Catholic family in Cork and ordained in 1906 (Borgonovo, 2017,

p. 123). Advancing through the nationalist wing of Ireland's cultural revival at the start of the twentieth century, he became friends with IRA leaders and participated in paramilitary activities, finding international attention as prison chaplain and spokesman for Terence MacSwiney's ten-week hunger strike in London's Brixton prison (Borgonovo, 2017, p. 125). The Turkish bath is plunged low with access granted by steps down into it. The audience encircle O'Conner as he looks up to them, as if to the heavens, acknowledging that he is now 'a man of god', but not a man 'of church' (*Hammam* show document, p. 22). He was informed by 'the Capuchin provincial that no bishop in Ireland will ever again grant me diocesan faculties' (p. 22). As he washes himself with the little water available, it is clear that the moment of water touching the boundary of his skin is perhaps the only respite left. Exiled by the religious organisation he had pledged his life to as a result of his continued involvement with the anti-Treaty rebellion, the water soothes his wounds. He is being reborn, as the dream of the Republic had promised, offering spiritual guidance to those remaining in the Hammam Hotel in what may be their final hours.

Hammam did not portray any glory in those final days. Rather, it revealed a biting loneliness for those refusing to surrender, unable to accept any future the Anglo-Irish Treaty might offer. The only comfort that arises is rooted in friendship amongst the women as they support each other's work in the hospital and political commitment to the cause, regardless of military orders for them to surrender. These women will not accept any more orders from male superiors that clash with their own instincts of what is right for them. In staging their final moments as occupying a position of agency and sisterhood, Lowe reveals her own feminist instincts and loyalties. She could have focused on the bombs, the white flags, and the political speeches, aligning with the majority of Irish historical narratives. Instead, she directed the audience gaze to Ireland's female revolutionaries who sacrificed their freedom, families and health in the pursuit of a future that sought equality for all, refusing to accept a 'stepping stone' in its place. In O'Rourke's review of *Hammam*, he refers to Lowe's extraordinary innovative body of work, concluding 'That the self-effacing Lowe hasn't yet been properly recognised, or elected to Aosdána, is not just a shame, it's an outright crime' (2023). That 'crime' was put to rights in spring 2024, as Lowe became inducted into Aosdána, Ireland's affiliation of creative artists founded in 1881 which 'honours artists whose work has made an outstanding contribution to the creative arts' (Aosdána, 2024). A recording of *Hammam* was made available to 'On Demand' through the Abbey Theatre website between 18 July and 8 August. Copies of the Show Documents are held by ANU, though the recorded performances offer greater immediacy, while still a very distinct experience from attending live.

3.4 Conclusion

For an Irish theatre artist, one could argue Lowe's creative practice is intensely un-Irish, yet the stories she tells are uniquely so. The modern Irish theatre tradition is inherently associated with the role of language in narrative storytelling, politics, and colonialism (Morash, 2002; Richards, 2004), while Lowe's work is fundamentally focused on the body as arbiter of meaning and mode of connection. Lowe's practice is evidently body-led, though she remains a playwright in many traditional ways as she writes the script. However, the script is a draft that operates as a map in rehearsals, edited and informed by creative producers, performers, designers, historians, stage managers, interns, and assistant directors (Haughton rehearsal notes, 2022; 2024). Such is the level of collaboration among the ensemble in crafting the performance that more than a week had passed in the rehearsals for *The Wakefires* before I realised Sinéad Diskin was not the dramaturg, but the composer.

Lowe's twenty-two major works with ANU, all sold out, have been staged during Ireland's Decade of Centenaries (DoC) with many co-sponsored by associated public funding awards. Not all were directly related to the DoC, but were staged in this moment of wider social commentary and reflection. This 'national' commemorative context in which her work has been conceived, produced, and received is essential to a wider understanding of Lowe's artistic intentions, trajectory, and legacy. What does 'national' mean on a small island with a large physical border, and arguably, an even larger psychological border? What does 'national' mean in relation to identity and experience post-Brexit, propelling significant momentum behind calls for Irish unity? Most significantly perhaps, what does 'national' mean when the commemorative agenda illustrates that the integrity and objectivity of many historical narratives of 'nation' are in dispute, with greater attention recently paid to the voices of those once relegated to the margins? The past cannot change, but one can learn it differently: this is what Lowe and ANU's theatrical practice has so deftly demonstrated, particularly through their focus on loaded sites of performance, immersive encounters, archival analysis, audience intimacy, and community interactions and inquiries.

In postcolonial contexts such as with the island of Ireland, and indeed through the commemoration of battles or wars, commemoration becomes inextricably linked with a remembrance of the loss of human life and a questioning of how histories were written. These tense, political, emotional, and often unresolved histories make certain structures of power more visible, further examined by Lowe through her techniques of audience immersivity and staging competing narratives that are not resolved by the end of the performance, allowing the insinuations, half-truths, and archival remnants to linger and fester. Diana Taylor's formulations in *The Archive and the Repertoire* propose a continual interrogation of the relationship between embodied performance and the production of knowledge. Her critique questions '[h]ow can we think about performance in historical terms, when the archive cannot capture and store the live event'? (2003, p. xvi) Lowe's major works with ANU negotiate this terrain. Taylor reinforces the significance of such analyses in its difficult and potentially flawed capacity, in claiming that '[if] performance did not transmit knowledge, only the literate and powerful could claim social memory and identity' (p. xviii).

In summary, Lowe's practice begins and ends with the body. From shadowing Lowe in rehearsals during *The Wakefires* and *Hammam*, Lowe's practice is intensely framed and contextualised by seminars with leading Irish historians, sociologists, military, and folklore experts. Through this research phase, Lowe supports performers in their selection of the individual they will embody for performance. The choreography of movement and dance work responds to the historical exploration of what may have been done to those bodies, and, in turn, what those bodies may have done to others. Finally, through a collision of historical enquiry, script, movement, and scenographic design at the site of performance, the ensemble led by Lowe propose ways for the performance to invite (but not enforce) a response from the audience. The absent body and silenced voice from the official record is what Lowe is most drawn to, recontextualising their lives, experiences, and legacies through ANU's 'NOW-THEN-NOW' overarching dramaturgical frame. In the context of her work developed and produced during Ireland's Decade of Centenaries, her practice is informed by, troubled with, and responds to, how the Irish state became formed and constituted in the twentieth century, and how the performance(s) of nationhood materialise in personal, familial, community, and national encounters.

In *The Performance of Nationalism*, Jisha Menon queries, '[c]an mimesis initiate a process of renewed world-making?' (2012, p. 18) The too painful past, which may not be as popular in commemorative agendas, can lose out in this potential world-making process that Menon unpacks. Histories that centralise the potential failure and victories of nationalism, nationhood and its related ideologies can be embroiled in a restaging for contemporary political purposes. Indeed, mimesis can often be used in the manipulation of memory and remembrance culture, rather than modes of examining the past. However, mimesis can also offer alternatives. Menon details that

> The transformation of painful past into aesthetic pleasure through mimetic practice depends on the capacity of the mimetic arts to offer a renewed understanding of the event. Whereas philosophy is concerned with abstract

universal, and history with contingent particular, poetry offers a sensuous understanding – at once concrete and contemplative – of the world we inhabit. (pp. 13–4)

Lowe's practice during this commemorative moment in Ireland responds to Menon's thinking here of 'a renewed understanding of the event'. Through her focus on 'ethical encounters' and 'moments of communion' (Lowe, 2012) staged at loaded sites, Lowe creates the potential for renewed understanding of Irish histories, 'confronting' (Crowe, 2023) or 'witnessing' (O'Carroll, 2023) the most painful and unresolved legacies of the past.

Lowe crafts performance encounters that directly engage with these ideological and historical spaces, in addition to the imaginary and creative realms of the interior self. She propels her audiences to journey through the private and the public, punctuating space in dominant narratives for other voices and bodies to emerge. 'I like women who know who they are,' she tells her ensemble as they review the tapestry of Irish female revolutionary experience (Haughton rehearsal notes, 2022) and these women are paid tribute in her body of work, if almost a century late.

References

Abbey Theatre: www.abbeytheatre.ie/.

Aiken, S. (2022a). *Spiritual Wounds: Trauma, Testimony and the Irish Civil War*. Dublin: Irish Academic Press.

  (2022b). Understanding the Trauma of the Irish Civil War. *The Irish Revolution Project*, University College Cork: www.ucc.ie/en/theirishrevolution/feature-articles/understanding-the-trauma-of-the-irish-civli-war-.html.

An Garda Síochána, Ireland's National Police and Security Service: www.garda.ie/en/

ANU Productions, 'Past Work': https://anuproductions.ie/past-work/.

  (2009) *Basin*.

  (2010, 2011) *World End's Lane*.

  (2011) *Laundry*.

  (2012) *The Boys of Foley Street*.

  (2013) *Living the Lockout*.

  (2013) *Thirteen*.

  (2014) *Vardo*.

  (2014) *Angel Meadow*.

  (2014) *Beautiful Dreamers*.

  (2015) *Pals: The Irish at Gallipoli*.

  (2016) *On Corporation Street*.

  (2016) *Rebel Rebel*.

  (2016) *Sunder*.

  (2016, 2018) *The Lost O'Casey*.

  (2016, 2018) *These Rooms*.

  (2017) *The Sin Eaters*.

  (2017) *Hentown*.

  (2019) *Faultline*.

  (2020) *The Party to End All Parties*.

  (2021) *The Book of Names*.

  (2022) *The Wakefires*.

  (2022, 2023) *Staging the Treaty*.

  (2023–4) *Hamman*.

Aosdána: http://aosdana.artscouncil.ie/.

Ayling, R. (1962). Nannie's Night Out. *Modern Drama*, **5**(2), 154–163.

BCC, (2022). Manchester IRA 1996 bomb: Man Released after Arrest. 10 September: www.bbc.com/news/uk-england-manchester-62862703.

Berry, L. M. (2009). Amazing Makeover that Turned Fair City's Una into Old Bag Lady. *Irish Independent*, 31 August: www.independent.ie/regionals/herald/amazing-makeover-that-turned-fair-citys-una-into-old-bag-lady/27923160.html.

Blain, E. (2008). An Honour Killing. *Irish Independent*, 5 June: www.independ ent.ie/regionals/herald/an-honour-killing/27874802.html.

Bliss, P. /O'Neill, R. (2020). Pantisocracy Interview with Louise Lowe. https://vimeo.com/442394234.

Borgonovo, J. (2017). The Exile and Repatriation of Father Dominic O'Connor (O. F. M. Capuchin), 1922–58. *Éire-Ireland*, **52**(3–4), 122–156.

Boss, O. (2024). Unpublished Interview with Miriam Haughton. Zoom, 30 January.

Brooklyn Academy of Music (BAM): www.bam.org/.

Cambridge Dictionary, (2023). 'Working-class' Definition: https://dictionary .cambridge.org/dictionary/english/working-class.

Clann. http://clannproject.org/about/.

CoisCéim Dance Theatre: https://coisceim.com/.

Coleman, M. (2017). Compensating Irish Female Revolutionaries, 1916–1923. *Women's History Review*, **27**(6), 915–934.

Connolly, L (2020). *Women and the Irish Revolution*. Dublin: Irish Academic Press.

   (2021). Ethical Commemoration, Women and the Irish Revolution 1919–23, *Machnamh 100*. Presidential Seminars, 150–151: https://president.ie/en/presidential-seminars/machnamh-100.

Cork Midsummer Festival: www.corkmidsummer.com/.

Crowe, C. (2023). Unpublished Interview with Miriam Haughton. Irish Theatre Institute Dublin, 23 October.

Dáil Éireann Debate, (1922). Debate on the Treaty 7 January. Dublin: Houses of the Oireachtas: www.oireachtas.ie/en/debates/debate/dail/1922-01-07/2/.

DeAngelis, T. (2019). The Legacy of Trauma. *American Psychological Association*, **50**(2), 36, www.apa.org/monitor/2019/02/legacy-trauma.

Delay, C. (2020). Death, Danger, and Decadence in 1920s Dublin: The Murder of Honor Bright. *Nursing Clio*, 7 January: https://nursingclio.org/2020/01/07/death-danger-and-decadence-in-1920s-dublin-the-murder-of-honor-bright/.

Department of Tourism, Culture, Arts, Gaeltacht, Sport and Media. Decade of Centenaries 2012–2023. www.decadeofcentenaries.com/about/.

Dublin City Council Blessington St Basin: www.dublincity.ie/residential/parks/dublin-city-parks/visit-park/blessington-street-basin.

Dublin Fringe Festival. (2009). Programme: https://issuu.com/dublinfringefes
tival/docs/fringe-2009.

Dublin Theatre Festival: https://dublintheatrefestival.ie/.

Elizabeth Fort: www.corkcity.ie/en/elizabeth-fort/history/.

Esslin, M. (1976). *An Anatomy of Drama*. London: T. Smith.

European Commission. Financial Assistance to Ireland: https://economy-
finance.ec.europa.eu/eu-financial-assistance/euro-area-countries/finan
cial-assistance-ireland_en.

Ferriter, D. (2015). *A Nation and Not a Rabble: The Irish Revolution 1913–
1922*. London: Profile Books.

(2022). *Between Two Hells: The Irish Civil War*. London: Profile Books.

Furlong, S. (2009–2010). 'Herstory' Recovered: Assessing the Contribution of
Cumann na mBan 1914–1923. *The Past*, **30**, 70–93.

Gate Theatre: https://www.gatetheatre.ie/.

Gillis, L. (2011). *The Fall of Dublin: 28 June to 5 July 1922*. Cork: Mercier
Press.

(2023). A Three Minute Guide to the Battle of Dublin. RTÉ, 2 March: www
.rte.ie/history/2023/0209/1355729-a-three-minute-guide-to-the-battle-of-
dublin/#:~:text=By%20Liz%20Gillis,key%20locations%20have%
20changed%20here.

Gilmartin, M. and Murphy, C. (2024). A Small Country with a Huge Diaspora,
Ireland Navigates its New Status as an Immigration Hub. Migration Policy
Institute, 5 June: www.migrationpolicy.org/article/ireland-diaspora-immi
gration#:~:text=This%20net%20emigration%20gave%20rise,Kingdom%
2C%20Canada%2C%20and%20Australia.

Gittins, E. (2022). The Fire at the Four Courts. Trinity College Dublin, 30 June:
www.tcd.ie/library/manuscripts/blog/2022/06/the-fire-at-the-four-courts/

Guerrilla Girls: www.guerrillagirls.com/.

Hanna, H. (1915). *Pals at Sulva Bay*. Royal Dublin Fusiliers: https://royaldu
blinfusiliers.com/books/pals-at-suvla-bay/.

Haraway, D. (1988). Situated Knowledges: The Science Question in
Feminism and the Privilege of Partial Perspective. *Feminist Studies*, **14**
(3), 575–599.

Haughton, M. (2014a). From Laundries to Labour Camps: Staging Ireland's
"Rule of Silence" in Anu Productions' Laundry. *Modern Drama*, **57**(1),
65–93.

(2014b). Mirror Mirror on the Wall: Unwanted Reflections in the Boys of
Foley Street. In T. Tracy and C. Holohan, Eds., *Masculinity and Irish
Popular Culture: Tiger's Tales*. Basingstoke: Palgrave, pp. 142–158.

(2021). *Legacies of the Magdalen Laundries: Commemoration, Gender and the Postcolonial Carceral State*. Eds., E. Pine and M. McAuliffe. Manchester: Manchester University Press.

(2022). Unpublished Rehearsal Notes, *The Wakefires* by ANU Productions with Cork Midsummer Festival. Dublin and Cork, May-June.

(2023). Unpublished Rehearsal Notes, *Hammam* by ANU Productions with the Abbey Theatre. Dublin, December.

Henriques, M. (2019). Can the Legacy of Trauma be Passed Down the Generations? BBC Future, 26 March: www.bbc.com/future/article/20190326-what-is-epigenetics.

HIA. Inquiry into Historical Institutional Abuse Inquiry in Northern Ireland between 1922 and 1995. www.hiainquiry.org/.

Hill, S. (2017). Feeling Out of Place: The 'affective dissonance' of the feminist spectator in the Boys of Foley Street. In E. Diamond, D. Varney, and C. Amich, Eds., *Performance, Feminism and Affect in Neoliberal Times*. Basingstoke: Palgrave, pp. 269–281.

Holdsworth, N. (2010). *Theatre and Nation*. Basingstoke: Palgrave.

HOME Manchester: https://homemcr.org/.

Hugh Lane Gallery, Dublin, Ireland: https://hughlane.ie/.

Irish Playography. Louise Lowe. Dublin: Irish Theatre Institute, https://irish playography.com/person?personid=40858.

JFMR. 'Justice for Magdalenes' was established in 2003, shifting to 'Justice for Magdalenes Research' in 2013 having achieved its aims of a State Apology and the establishment of a commission to create a Redress Scheme. http://jfmresearch.com/.

Jones, Rev Simon. 'Holy Week: Last Supper and Footwashing'. Oxford: Merton College, www.merton.ox.ac.uk/socially-isolated-spiritually-con nected/holy-week-last-supper-and-footwashing#:~:text=On%20the% 20night%20before%20his,I%20have%20done%20to%20you'.

Joye, L. (2024). Unpublished Interview with Miriam Haughton. Irish Film Institute Dublin, 20 April.

Joye, L. and Lowe, L. (2015). PALS – the Irish in Gallipoli. *Museum Ireland*, **25**, Dublin: Irish Museums Association, 137–145.

Kavanagh, Ú. (2024). Unpublished Interview with Miriam Haughton. Irish Theatre Institute, Dublin, 9 February.

(2009). *Black Bessie*, Merrion Square Park, 14–19 September, Dublin Fringe Festival: https://issuu.com/dublinfringefestival/docs/fringe-2009.

Kavanagh, Ú. and Lowe, L. (2017). The Work of ANU: The Audience is Present. *Irish University Review*, **47**(1), 119–125.

Keating, S. (2009). What Site-Specific Really Means. *Irish Theatre Magazine*, 26 September: http://itmarchive.ie/web/Features/Current/What-site-spe cific-really-means.aspx.html.

Kelly, M., O'Gorman, S., and Phillips, Á. (2020). Performing Ireland: Now, then, Now . . . . *Scene*, **8**, 1–116.

Kristeva, J. and Lechte, J. (1982). Approaching Abjection. *Oxford Literary Review*, **5**(1–2), 125–149.

Landmark Productions: www.landmarkproductions.ie/.

Lanters, J. (2021). 'Dragging our Hidden Slums into the Centre of the Footlights': Homelessness, Addiction and Audience Discomfort in Sean O'Casey's Nannie's Night Out and ANU's The Lost O'Casey. *New Hibernia Review*, **25**(2), 60–75.

Leland, M. (2022). A daughter sexually assaulted by Black and Tans, a 'parcel of bombs' in a woman's pocket. *Irish Times*, 8 June: www.irishtimes.com/ culture/stage/2022/06/08/a-daughter-sexually-assaulted-by-a-gang-of-black-and-tans-a-parcel-of-bombs-in-a-womans-pocket/.

Little, J. (2020). Reframing the Politics of Performance at 14 Henriette Street: ANU's Living the Lockout and Company SJ's Fizzles. *Text and Performance Quarterly*, **40**(4), 343–363.

London International Festival of Theatre: www.liftfestival.com/.

Lowe, L. (2012). Unpublished Interview with Miriam Haughton. Dublin, 15 May.

(2013). In Conversation with Patrick Lonergan. Synge Summer School. Co. Wicklow.

(2020). Unpublished Interview with Miriam Haughton. Zoom, 2 September.

(2021a). Unpublished Interview with Miriam Haughton, Dublin, 10 August.

(2021b). *The Wakefires* Show Document.

(2023). *Hammam* Show Document.

(2024). Unpublished Interview with Miriam Haughton. Zoom, 29 April.

Lowe, L. and Boss, O. (2005) *Tumbledowntown*. Produced by Roundabout Theatre as part of the Dublin Fringe Festival. Programme: https://issuu .com/dublinfringefestival/docs/fringe-2005/14.

Lowe, L. and Boss, O. (2021). University of Galway Webinar. Zoom, 18 February.

(2023). Unpublished Interview with Miriam Haughton. Zoom, 17 August.

Lowe, L. and Haughton, M. (2025). Loss. In J. Moran, (ed.), *Sean O'Casey in Context*. Cambridge University Press, pp. 201–215.

Lowe, W. J. (2004). 'Who were the Black-and-tans?' *History Ireland*, **12**(3): www.historyireland.com/who-were-the-black-and-tans/.

MacKillop, J. (2004). Anu in a Dictionary of Celtic Mythology. Oxford Reference online: www.oxfordreference.com/display/10.1093/acref/9780

198609674.001.0001/acref-9780198609674-e-189?rskey=IvLFcP
&result=189.

Malekmian, S. (2023). On a Quiet South Dublin Road, a Plaque Serves as a Reminder of a Long Unsolved Murder. *Dublin Inquirer*, 30 August: https://dublininquirer.com/2023/08/30/on-a-quiet-south-dublin-road-a-plaque-serves-as-a-reminder-of-a-long-unsolved-murder/.

McAuliffe, M. (2022). Commemorating Women's Histories during the Irish Decade of Centenaries. *Éire-Ireland*, **57**, 237–259.

The Wakefires Programme Note, Cork Midsummer Festival: https://www.cork midsummer.com/content/files/Wakefires-v2.pdf.

(2023). The Treatment of Militant Anti-Treaty Women in Kerry by the National Army during the Irish Civil War. *Éire-Ireland*, **58**, 72–100.

McCann, N. (2022). Out of the Ashes – Ireland's Archives Reborn. BBC News NI, 28 June: www.bbc.com/news/uk-northern-ireland-61955762.

McGettrick, C., O'Donnell, K., Smith, J. O'Rourke, M., and Steed, M. (2021). *Ireland and the Magdalene Laundries: A Campaign for Justice*. London: I. B. Tauris.

Menon, J. (2013). *The Performance of Nationalism: India, Pakistan and the memory of partition*. Cambridge: Cambridge University Press.

Military Archives, Military Service Pensions Collection 1916–1923: www .militaryarchives.ie/collections/online-collections/military-service-pen sions-collection-1916–1923.

Mná 100: www.mna100.ie/about-mna-100/.

Morash, C. (2002). *A History of Irish Theatre 1601–2000*. Cambridge: Cambridge University Press.

Mountjoy Female Prison, Irish Prison Service: www.irishprisons.ie/prison/doc has-centre/.

Mullally, U. (2023). *Hammam* Review: Louise Lowe's Terrifying Immersive Play Reinforces Anu's Singular Position in Irish Theatre. *Irish Times*, 24 December: www.irishtimes.com/culture/stage/review/2023/12/24/ham mam-review-louise-lowes-terrifying-immersive-play-reinforces-anus-sin gular-position-in-irish-theatre/.

Murphy, C. L. (2023). *Performing Social Change on the Island of Ireland: From Republic to Pandemic*. London: Routledge.

Murray, C. (1997). *Twentieth-Century Irish Drama: Mirror up to Nation*. Manchester: Manchester University Press.

National Museum of Ireland. The Signing of the Anglo-Irish Treaty 1921: www .museum.ie/en-IE/Collections-Research/Collection/Documentation-Discoveries/Artefact/The-Signing-of-the-Anglo-Irish-Treaty,-1921/ 7a49e7e5-7cf7-4218-b3b4-c974d4adafa6.

O'Carroll, A. (2018). Programme note for *The Lost O'Casey*, written and directed by Lowe, produced by ANU Productions as part of the Dublin Theatre Festival.

(2023). Unpublished Interview with Miriam Haughton. Zoom, 14 November.

O'Casey, S. (1924). *Nannie's Night Out* in *Feathers from the Green Crow: Sean O'Casey 1905–1925*. (Ed.) Robert Hogan. Columbia, MO: University of Missouri Press 1962.

1945 *Drums under the Windows*. London: Macmillan.

Ó Corráin, D. and Hanley, G. (2022a). The Battle for Dublin's O'Connell Street 100 years Ago this Week. RTÉ Brainstorm, 5 July: www.rte.ie/brainstorm/2022/0705/1308469-irish-civil-war-dublin-oconnell-street-july-1922/#:~:text=The%20Hammam%20Hotel%20was%20shelled,breach%20with%20Lewis%20machine%2Dguns.

(2022b). Cathal Brugha: An 'extraordinary' life cut short by the Civil War. RTÉ Brainstorm, 7 July: www.rte.ie/brainstorm/2022/0706/1308779-cathal-brugha-civil-war-july-1922-irish-revolution/.

(2022c). *Cathal Brugha: 'An Indomitable Spirit'*. Dublin: Four Courts Press.

O'Keeffe, H. Mapping the Burning of Cork 11–12 December 1920. The Irish Revolution Project, Cork: University College Cork: www.ucc.ie/en/theirishrevolution/collections/mapping-the-irish-revolution/mapping-the-burning-of-cork-11-december-1920/.

Ó Murchadha, C. (2011). *The Great Famine: Ireland's Agony, 1845–1852*. New York: Continuum.

One in Four. www.oneinfour.ie/.

O'Rourke, C. (2023). Hammam. *The Arts Review*, 23 December: www.theartsreview.com/single-post/hammam#:~:text=Blisteringly%20brilliant%20in%20all%20imaginable,sent%20off%20on%20opposing%20paths.

O'Sullivan, E. and O'Donnell, I. (2012). *Coercive Confinement in Post-Independence Ireland: Patients, Prisoners and Penitents*. Manchester: Manchester UP.

O'Toole, E. (2018). The Church Brutalised Ireland. *The Guardian*, 9 July: www.theguardian.com/commentisfree/2018/jul/09/catholic-church-ireland-pope-francis-visit-abuse.

O'Toole, F. (2016). Ballymun at 50: From High Hopes to Sink Estate. *Irish Times*, 23 July: www.irishtimes.com/life-and-style/people/ballymun-at-50-from-high-hopes-to-sink-estate-1.2731512.

Pierse, M. (Ed.) (2017). *A History of Irish Working-Class Writing*. Cambridge: Cambridge University Press.

(2020). Ireland's Working-Class Literature: Neglected Themes, Amphibian Academics and the Challenges Ahead. *Irish University Review*, **50**(1), 67–81.

Radak, T. (2023). (Un)real City: Spatial and Temporal Ghosting in ANU Productions' the Party to End All Parties. *Journal of Contemporary Drama in English*, **11**(1), 39–58.

Renoir, Pierre-Auguste. *Les Parapluies/The Umbrellas*. The National Gallery, London: www.nationalgallery.org.uk/paintings/pierre-auguste-renoir-the-umbrellas.

Richards, S, (Ed.) (2004). *The Cambridge Companion to Twentieth-Century Irish Drama*. Cambridge University Press.

RTÉ Archives. (1972). Scourge of Drug Addiction: www.rte.ie/archives/2017/0925/907320-heroin-use-in-ireland/.

Schneider, R. (1997). *The Explicit Body in Performance*. Routledge.

Screen Ireland: www.screenireland.ie/.

Singleton, B. (2016). *ANU Productions: The Monto Cycle*. Basingstoke: Palgrave.

(2021a). Holding the Queer Irish Archive: An Interview with Louise Lowe and Lynnette Moran on ANU Productions' Faultline. *Contemporary Theatre Review*, **31**(1–2), 204–211.

(2021b). ANU Productions and the Performance of Otherness. *Orbis Litterarum*, **76**, 301–310.

Smith, J. (2007). *Ireland's Magdalen Laundries and the Nation's Architecture of Containment*. Indiana: Notre Dame University Press.

Snyder-Young, D. (2013). *Theatre of Good Intentions: Challenges and Hopes for Theatre and Social Change*. Basingstoke: Palgrave.

Taylor, D. (2003). *The Archive and the Repertoire: Performing Cultural Memory in the Americas*. Durham, NC: Duke University Press.

Till, K. (2018). 'Waiting for the City to Remember': Archive and Repertoire in ANU's These Rooms. *The Irish Review*, **54**, 34–51.

Tuam Oral History Project 2019–2023: www.universityofgalway.ie/tuam-oral-history/.

Wheatfield Prison, Irish Prison Service: www.irishprisons.ie/prison/wheatfield-place-of-detention/.

Acknowledgements

It has been a privilege to write this Element and only made possible due to the generosity of Louise Lowe. For over a decade, I have been intrigued by how she tells stories, particularly those of historical figures in Ireland who were mistreated, marginalised, or omitted from records. As I journey through her body of work, I receive the missing pieces of a vital education in Irish history and feminist politics necessary to understand on what ground I stand, and how I got here.

My gratitude in this regard is extended to Ciaran Bagnall, Owen Boss, Stephen Bourke, Ghaliah Conroy, Leanna Cuttle, Sinéad Diskin, Darragh Feehely, Kate Finnegan, Ella Lily Hyland, Úna Kavanagh, Maree Kearns, Rob Moloney, Lynnette Moran, Sarah Morris, Robbie O'Connor, Saileóg O'Halloran, Jamie O'Neill, Peter Rothwell, Matt Smyth, Eftychia Spyridaki, Matthew Williamson, and everyone involved with ANU Productions. Thank you for sharing your ideas. Inviting in non-company members to observe rehearsals at such nascent and vulnerable moments of the creative process is no small thing. It was the most exciting creative and critical space to be in, and I salute the endless energy and commitment each of you dedicates to your work.

My sincere thanks also to those individuals who provided me with interviews, research materials, and support to enable this Element to find its voice, especially Owen Boss, Catriona Crowe, Lar Joye, Úna Kavanagh, Cathy Leeney, Louise Lowe, Brenda Malone, Austin O'Carroll, and Brian Singleton. If this work offers even a crumb of your intelligence, empathy, and analytical prowess, then I will rest easy.

To all at Cambridge University Press, in particular, Emily Hockley, George Laver, and Series Editors Elaine Aston, and Melissa Sihra, I am very grateful for your support. Your guidance and patience enabled this Element to materialise despite a pandemic, illness, bereavement, and all the false starts that go with the territory.

I must also express my gratitude to the University of Galway for their commitment to arts research and sponsoring the gold open-access publication of this work. To my colleagues in the College of Arts, Social Sciences and Celtic Studies, the School of English, Media and Creative Arts, and the Discipline of Drama and Theatre Studies, thank you for the collegiality, support, and understanding while I found my way to the finish line.

Many of the ideas of this book were first tested out in the annual conferences of the Irish Society for Theatre Research (ISTR) and the Feminist Working Group of the International Federation for Theatre Research (IFTR), and my thanks to all my colleagues in those networks for their rigorous engagement and supportive feedback.

This Element is dedicated to my parents Mary and Robert, who would have loved to have been here to celebrate it.

Cambridge Elements ☰

Women Theatre Makers

Elaine Aston
Lancaster University
Elaine Aston is internationally acclaimed for her feminism and theatre research. Her monographs include *Caryl Churchill* (1997); *Feminism and Theatre* (1995); *Feminist Theatre Practice* (1999); *Feminist Views on the English Stage* (2003); and *Restaging Feminisms* (2020). She has served as Senior Editor of Theatre Research International (2010–12) and President of the International Federation for Theatre Research (2019–23).

Melissa Sihra
Trinity College Dublin
Melissa Sihra is Associate Professor in Drama and Theatre Studies at Trinity College Dublin. She is author of *Marina Carr: Pastures of the Unknown* (2018) and editor of *Women in Irish Drama: A Century of Authorship and Representation* (2007). She was President of the Irish Society for Theatre Research (2011–15), and is currently researching a feminist historiography of the Irish playwright and co-founder of the Abbey Theatre, Lady Augusta Gregory.

About the Series
This innovative, inclusive series showcases women-identifying theatre makers from around the world. Expansive in chronological and geographical scope, the series encompasses practitioners from the late nineteenth century onwards and addresses a global, comprehensive range of creatives – from playwrights and performers to directors and designers.

Cambridge Elements ≡

Women Theatre Makers

Elements in the Series

Maya Rao and Indian Feminist Theatre
Bishnupriya Dutt

Xin Fengxia and the Transformation of China's Ping Opera
Siyuan Liu

Emma Rice's Feminist Acts of Love
Lisa Peck

Women Making Shakespeare in the Twenty-First Century
Kim Solga

Clean Break Theatre Company
Caoimhe McAvinchey, Sarah Bartley, Deborah Dean and Anne-marie Greene

#WakingTheFeminists and the Data-Driven Revolution in Irish Theatre
Claire Keogh

The Theatre of Louise Lowe
Miriam Haughton

A full series listing is available at: www.cambridge.org/EWTM

Printed in the United States
by Baker & Taylor Publisher Services